THANK GOD
I'm a Teenager

New, Revised Edition

THANK GOD
I'm a Teenager

CHARLES S. MUELLER
DONALD R. BARDILL

AUGSBURG Publishing House • Minneapolis

THANK GOD I'M A TEENAGER
New, Revised Edition

Scripture quotations unless otherwise noted are from the Holy Bible: New International Version. Copyright 1978 by the New York International Bible Society. Used by permission of Zondervan Bible Publishers.

First published in 1976 by Augsburg Publishing House.

Library of Congress Cataloging-in-Publication Data

Mueller, Charles S.
    Thank God I'm a teenager / Charles S. Mueller and Donald R.
Bardill.—New, rev. ed.
        p.   cm.
    Summary: Advice for gaining personal maturity as a Christian
during the teenage years.
    ISBN 0-8066-2351-9
    1. Adolescence—Juvenile literature.   2. Teenagers—Conduct of
life—Juvenile literature.   3. Christian life—Juvenile literature.
[1. Christian life.]   I. Bardill, Donald R.   II. Title.
HQ796.M8325   1988
170'.2'0223—dc 19   88-6215
                                                                        CIP
                                                                         AC

Manufactured in the U.S.A.   APH 10-6242

1   2   3   4   5   6   7   8   9   0   1   2   3   4   5   6   7   8   9

CONTENTS

ABOUT THIS BOOK

If anyone ever gets around to selecting a patron saint for teenagers, I have a great nominee: Christopher Columbus. Don't ask me how "saintly" old Chris was. His moral conduct, no matter how great it might have been, isn't the basis for my suggestion. I chose him because of the intriguing similarity between his unexpected and unanticipated discovery of America and the equally unexpected and unanticipated discoveries that come to all who set sail from the safety of 12 years of age toward the unknown world of 20. One man described Chris's experience this way: "He didn't know where he was going when he left; he didn't know where he was when he got there; he didn't know where he had been when he had returned." Sound familiar, and maybe a little frightening? If that's the kind of uncertain journey you have to look forward to during the teenage years, who needs it?

Whether you need it or not isn't the question. The fact is that you're going to go through those seven remarkable years day-by-day and year-by-year until finally they are behind you. No matter how tightly you squeeze shut your eyes, or how strenuously you try to avoid the experience, the teenage years just won't go away. No one has invented a magic carpet for whisking people across those years overnight. Everybody, and I mean everybody, is going to work their way through those seven years of growing up and one way or another make it to the end.

Does that sound negative? It's almost as if I were talking about a bitter-tasting medicine that has to be endured. The teenage years aren't like that at all. They are glorious and glowing, wondrous and exciting, filled with all kinds of adventures. That's how they will be for anyone who makes preparation, and who wants to enjoy these good years.

It's not too late for you to prepare for your journey toward that magic goal of 20. And it's not too early, either. It's just the right time, because it's your time. Even if a few of those teen years have already slipped by, you can still decide to make the rest of them some of the best of your life. Making those years the best is what this book is all about.

Two authors worked together to write this book. One is a clinical social worker with 20 years of experience in counseling and family care. The other is a pastor with 25 years of service to people of all ages. Both of us are married and parents of teenagers. Both of us have frequent contacts with youth from coast to coast, in large and small gatherings, in retreats, classes, discussion groups, counseling sessions, and conversations.

This book includes ideas we have learned from personal experiences, insights we gained from the behavioral sciences, and thoughts from the Word of God.

In the book you will see that we have merged our identities and become an "I." The pronoun *I* makes the book easier to read, and besides, after months of working together our process of thinking has become unified.

How will this book be most useful?

Read the whole book. Underline and make notes along the way.

Invite your friends to form a discussion group.

Now we are ready to begin. And where shall we begin? At the beginning, of course!

1976

A P.S. for this revised edition

Over 10 years have passed since the first printing of this book. Life as a teenager in the late 1980s and early 1990s is quite different from life as a teenager in the late 1970s. Changes have taken place in our world since the '70s. They directly influence your daily life. For instance, while going to the movies is still fun, bringing the movies home to play on the VCR is also enjoyable. The computer has given us opportunities in areas not yet discovered or imagined. It is truly an exciting time for all of us, especially young people.

Many of you are experiencing other changes that are taking place in our society. The meaning of the "family" has changed. More mothers and teenagers work outside of the home nowadays. In contrast to the past, the economic forces of today's world are pulling all of us away from the family as the center of life. Members of the "modern" family spend more and more time in interests outside the family. There are ball games, tennis lessons, part-time jobs—all taking place outside the home. Of themselves these things are not new. But the volume of them! And the economic changes that allow us to do things which just a few years ago most families could not afford! Did you know that less than 10% of modern families regularly have a sit-down dinner together? All of us still eat. It just seems we eat at different times and in different places. We eat dinner in shifts and at all hours responding to our individual schedules.

Other changes have taken place in the family. There is an increasing number of blended, or reconstituted families in which a divorced parent marries another divorced parent. Sometimes these parents each have children of their own—a blend of *your-family*, *my-family* and *our-family*. Many of you reading this book may be living in a blended family. Blended families can do very well together.

Since the late 1970s there has been a rather dramatic increase in the number of single-parent families. Over one quarter of the teenagers reading this book have only one parent at home. In the years to come the percentage of single parent families in the United States is likely to increase even more. Just as with all different family makeups some teenagers do very well in a single-parent situation while others feel a lot of stress.

The peer pressure on teenagers of years ago has been made even more intense for your generation by the additional new pressures from the media and from the models for adult behavior provided by many parents. You cannot help but feel the influence of the increased sexual innuendos of television and movies. The incidence of sexually explicit lyrics to the music directed to your age group is on the increase. The message of the media is "everybody's doing it and you should, too." The recent emergence of AIDS as a life-threatening disease has clearly changed the sexual habits of people of all age groups. Many parents seem too busy with work or other activities to give much time to their families. The parental models often show very busy adults, many of whom are divorced, struggling through life under intense pressure. Evidence that some of your age group have yielded to the pressures of society shows in such behaviors as drug abuse, suicide, anorexia nervosa (starving yourself into a skeleton-like appearance, or death), alcohol abuse, extreme conformism to peer pressure, and much else.

It is a tribute to your age group that, in spite of all the pressures of the "modern" world, most teenagers make it through the 12 to 20 years without "stressing out" or losing their perspective.

While there have been many changes in our society over the past 10 years, the basic tasks of the teenage years discussed in this book have remained much the same. It is a time for growth, change, different choices, and excitement—enjoy it! Say it: "Thank God I'm a teenager."

1988

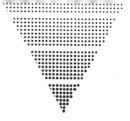

One

WHAT'S GOING ON HERE?

What's the first thing you do in the morning as you prepare for school? For most teens the first conscious act is a look in the mirror. You, too? Do you check your hair? (Is it combed your way?) What about your teeth? Sparkling? And your face—is it clean? Is that your morning routine? I'll bet it is. We all want to start out looking our best.

That same systematic approach makes sense for anyone moving out on the teenage adventure. So check. Start now. Take a good look at yourself. Review your appearance. Evaluate your personality. Consider your mannerisms and all the other things that, together, add up to *you*. After you have studied yourself—carefully—you will be able to make an informed judgment of what you see.

Right off the top of your head—I mean right now—what's your opinion? Do you like what you see? Don't cheat by letting someone else give you the answer to that question or con you into accepting their judgment. Don't let "them" push on you their idea of what a proper self-image should be, either. Make your own judgment about yourself. Draw your own conclusions. Those who do that discover there is no one in the whole world quite like them.

Does that depress you? You say you just spent $15 on a haircut so you could look just like your best friend? You say you're wearing a school jacket identical to those of your pals so that all the other guys will think you are just like them? You say you are breaking your back to be the mirror image of every other kid at school? And now I say that won't work because you are *distinctively you?* Yep. That's true.

I'll concede that in many ways you're very similar to your friends. That's not all bad. *But you aren't identical.* You are unique. There's no one else exactly like you. Those differences you notice, great and small, put you in a class all by yourself. You are uniquely you.

All that really means is that you aren't closed in by anyone else's limitations. That in turn, among other things, means you don't have to do what everyone else does. And there's more. No one has eyes quite like yours, or a body quite like yours, or a mind quite like yours, or a family quite like yours, or a school quite like yours. You, and all the "you-things" that surround you, added together, make up the very different and very special person that is you. That's wonderful. Be glad about it.

Unique, but not first

While you study yourself, be ready to realize that as a new (or older) teenager you aren't embarking on a pioneer's wandering into the uncharted seas of a fogged-in tomorrow. Others, before, have successfully made the trip from 12 to 20. Their journey, while not identical, was very similar. And other "others" are making an almost identical trip right now. Though you may feel you are making the journey by yourself, remember that billions (did you note the *b?*) have successfully covered that same eight-year adventure before you. Would you believe it—your parents, your teachers, your older brothers and sisters have made the teenage trip, blazed a trail, and even prepared valuable "maps" to help you know where you are, some places you ought to go, and how to get there safely.

If there are days you feel like a confused, 20th-century Christopher Columbus, that's understandable. You both have much in common. But there are also important differences between you and your friend, Chris. Let me cite two:

1. He sailed into a vast unknown with no real help available except his own convictions. Not so with you. You are actually sailing through some well-charted seas.

2. He bobbed across the Atlantic with no one else around except the nervous company of two or three even smaller ships. It's different with you. You are moving along as part of a mass of humanity, past and present, who partner with you in that great and exciting journey through the teens. Others can, and some surely will, help you. So sail on! In confidence.

A time for growing

The Bible records a preteen story about Jesus in Luke 2. He was 12 moving toward 13. It's the only story about him from birth to the beginning of his public ministry. Pay attention. There must be a reason God led the gospel writer to retell this one incident. Remember the details? Jesus had made a trip—a religious pilgrimage—to Jerusalem with his parents. While in the city he was separated from his mother and father. Heading back to Nazareth, their home town, they realized that Jesus was not with them. Was he lost? Had he been kidnapped? Was he maybe lying in a ditch, injured? Could he be dead?

The story turns out OK. After three days of separation the family was reunited. They had a moment of family conflict (See—it happens to the best!) before they closed ranks and, together, returned as a unit to their Nazareth home. Luke concludes the story with a very important statement, one that can help you understand some of what is happening to you as you move past 12 toward 13, 14, 15, and beyond: "And Jesus grew in wisdom and stature, and in favor with God and men" (Luke 2:52). Concentrate on the third word in the quotation. I mean "grew." *Grow* means more than "get bigger." The

13

meaning of that word which Luke was led to choose is, "cut a passage forward" (like hacking your way through the jungle underbrush with a machete), or "beat into useful shape" (like a silversmith pounding a chunk of metal into the form of a bracelet or ring). Growing means something like, "make a serious effort," or "try very hard." It isn't easy to grow. And it isn't automatic. When you're growing in the sense of Luke's special word you're going to get beat about a bit. You will have to muscle up for the hacking that's required for forward movement. But growing brings important results to your life. Like Jesus you will develop physically (he grew in stature), intellectually (grow in wisdom), spiritually and socially (grow in favor with God and man). How good you get at growing will predict the rate and the quality of the changes that take place in you and your life. As you get better at it you'll also discover that successful growing makes the eight years flow smoother. It even adds fun. And, as an expert grower, you'll be ready to successfully confront the *three phases* of the teen years that come to everyone, ready or not.

Three phases

There are three distinct phases in the teenage period. The exact time-boundary of these phases will vary from person to person, but generally they can be divided into *the early teens* (years 12, 13, and 14), *the middle teens* (from 15 to about 17), and—you guessed it—*the late teens* (from 17 on). In the early teenage years you often wonder, "Who am I going to be?" Around 15 you start asking, "Who am I now?" And at the end of the last period, somewhere around 19 or 20, you ask, "Who was I?" That's true!

The speed with which you move from one phase to another makes the teenager years both exciting and somewhat bewildering. The beginning of each phase is often marked by graduation from school: first, from elementary school at around 12, then, from junior high school at around 14 or 15, and finally from senior high at around 17 or 18. And you know what any graduation means! It means you start anew—and always at the bottom. About the time you become a wise sixth grader, and know how to run the elementary school, you graduate and start out as a dumb seventh grader in junior high! It's not fair. And when you have junior high whipped, and really know how to handle it, you get shot up to the bottom rung of senior high. That's how growing goes. However, every time you graduate and start again it's not as tough as it was before because with each new change you bring the experiences you have accumulated in the previous period of your life.

Something else is happening all the while too. You are changing.

Your changing mind

Some of us in recent years have worried about the long-term effects of "mind-expanding" drugs like LSD and other hallucinogenic compounds. While the teenage years are not a drug, they are very mind expanding. For instance, did you know that between the 12th and 15th year your mind actually begins to make radical shifts, to change and expand? All early teens develop an increased ability to consider new concepts, and consider them in ways that they couldn't before. You'll experience nostalgia and discover that you like watching cartoons and good movies from your childhood—but not for the same reason they once attracted you.

You get involved in interesting conversations about subjects you avoided only a few years ago. Without being fully conscious of it, your ability to reason logically increases dramatically. New interests develop. You may even come to the shocking realization that you actually like school—and poetry—or chemistry—and other equally unlikely things. And more. Little kids are able to let two things that are absolutely illogical stand side by side and think nothing of it. But by 15 you discover you have to struggle with those illogical opposites.

You want to resolve them one way or another or understand them or at least discuss them.

Something is happening. Actually, the knowledge you packed into your head in elementary school, plus other things you picked up outside the classroom, have been expanding your mind. You are developing an ability to use your accumulated knowledge to bring order in the face of conflicting ideas.

On the strange side of this kind of mind-expanding change, you discover that you begin to entertain new, exciting, sometimes frightening, and maybe even previously forbidden thoughts. They come at you so suddenly you don't even know where they come from. Some will be sexual; some will be what you always considered wrong; some will be so gross that you can hardly talk about them with your best friend.

Have you ever had a new thought and imagined you were the first person who has ever tied a series of bits and pieces of information together in the way you have? That's normal in the earliest teens. So much is going on in your head! Those early years are a time of great discovery. One great discovery: you can work things out, all by yourself, *in your head!* True. It happens. It has happened, or will happen, to you. Don't worry about this new stuff. It's great!

Daydreaming

Have you noticed that you daydream more during the teenage years? While daydreaming may be dangerous if you're doing it as you cross a busy street, it's not all bad—usually it's not even bad at all. In fact, daydreaming can be good. Through daydreaming you live through experiences you've never had. First you vividly imagine a circumstance in which you find yourself, and then you just as vividly imagine what you would do to get out of it. Through daydreaming you actually give shape to the direction you would like your life to go and the style in which you would like to live. As time goes by, you'll abandon the more exaggerated dimension of those dreams. But don't throw them overboard too soon. If you don't have the daydreams first, you'll never have anything to abandon. And don't worry: your increasingly logical mind will help you control daydreaming.

What if you tend to wander around in a perpetual dreamy-eyed fog? There'll always be someone who will thump you on your head, bring you up short, and draw you back to the realities of life. So do a little daydreaming. Go ahead. Think about what it would be like to ask that cute girl down the street for a kiss. Imagine you have just won the state beauty contest. Work through how you'd act if you were asked to star in the school play. It's all right. Make your daydreaming a kind of practice for life. That's what it really is. Keep an occasional ear cocked to the warnings of those about you so you don't go overboard! With that caution you'll find the experience of daydreaming both pleasant and helpful.

Good-bye baby fat

While things are going on inside your head, other stuff is going on in the rest of your body. You are changing physically. Baby fat begins to disappear and all kinds of new and (for both men and women) interesting muscles develop.

Did you know that a male's muscle strength doubles between his 12th and 16th years? He actually becomes twice as strong. A few months linked together makes a big difference. Yesterday's patsy can be tomorrow's ox! So look out. Be careful whom you bully. Before you know it, he may come back and pound you into the ground.

The muscle change in girls is not quite as dramatic as that in boys, but it's there, nonetheless. And there are other equally significant physical changes. You begin to develop the figure of a young woman. And both young men and young women begin growing hair on surprising areas of their bodies. Both experience pleasantly odd sensations. These new feelings can

17

be confusing because not many adults seem ready to explain them. The only thing adults (parents, too) seem to do by way of help is clear their throats a lot, make confusing comments about birds and bees, and issue veiled warnings.

In the early teens, and at about the same time, boys and girls experience a marked increase in their capacity for coordinated movement. Girls usually get there first. But for both, clumsiness disappears. They discover they can dance with the grace of a professional—or at least that's how it feels. They can run farther, swim faster, type quicker, and do all kinds of muscular things at an increased level of efficiency and effectiveness.

There are significant emotional changes too. Boys begin to think that maybe girls aren't so strange after all and shouldn't necessarily be avoided. Girls realize there is more to be said about members of the opposite sex than they are "dumb." Both may even suspect that they have the physical tools to translate their new feelings into human responses. People have all kinds of names to describe what's happening, but the simplest truth is that you are discovering you are a sexual person. That's not bad. It's part of God's great plan for your growing.

Life's seasoning

The day you realize that you are a sexual person is a great day. Sexuality adds flavoring and a glorious, God-given dimension to life. It's an early signal of the ripened richness coming. Like salt for food, sexuality enhances and seasons your appreciation for life and living.

Your time of growing in sexual sensitivity signals another major teenage task: developing your moral principles while expanding your caring capacity. Learning how to be close with another human being, and how to be close in a way that doesn't hurt the other or you, is a special ability. How long does that take? It actually requires all your teenage years—and the life-time that follows. The specific skill? I call the skill, "learning not to use one another."

In one sense the three words—"using one another"—are the most obscene in the English language. Before you will do anything immoral, unchaste, or improper with or to another human being, you first decide to use them. That means you turn the other person into a thing and forget about the effect of your action on him or her. Your interest is in what the person can do for you. Using someone else sometimes causes the person injury and is always a moral wrong.

Rape or physical abuse are obvious examples of using. A less obvious example would be going to a dance with a guy you can't stand because it's the only way to get there. You are "using" him. True? Or, if you date a girl just to prove to the guys that you can, even though you don't really care about her, then you are "using" her. True? And if you have sexual relations with someone just because you got all excited and have no intention or ability to accept the responsibilities for what you are doing, then someone is using someone. True? We'll get a lot more specific about all that in later chapters. For now let's press on with this overview.

Tough choices

A significant part of discovering yourself and expanding your horizons is developing the ability to make tough choices. Tough choices are coming. Some are already here. Your developing body and your new, exciting mind will force you to make decisions you've never had to make before. But your body and your mind can also help you. First, they will help you learn control. Maturing means your body and your mind are moving toward full growth. Second, maturing makes for becoming a real person—one who is whole. Whether you are there or not—that's your goal: wholeness. That, too, will be more completely presented in a later chapter. Control, maturing, wholeness all imply choices. When you merely give in to impulse, you have made no choice. You are not responding then. You are reacting. But as you face choices and make them in the fear of God and for love of others, life's best doors open and you grow more each day.

Your own pace

Not everyone will develop at the same speed. Young people don't develop at the same rate mentally, intellectually, sexually, socially, physically or any other way you can imagine. If you think you are lagging behind in one area or another, don't let it get you down. Believe me, late bloomers do bloom. Move at your own pace. Enjoy every minute of what you are, because one thing is certain: you won't remain that way very long. If you don't muscle out as fast as someone else or you don't have the figure of another your age, don't let it bother you. You are a "you." Everyone moves at an individualized pace. It's enough to know you are moving. Don't look down on yourself if you think you're going too slow. Don't look down on others who are coming along slower than you in any area (or up to others who seem to be whizzing along in life's fast lane!). Be thankful for the way God made you. Recognize that you are different from others and that others are different from you. Then move out down life's way—at your pace.

How to handle mistakes

Many contend Christopher Columbus actually made a mistake on his famous 1492 voyage. They say he landed in the wrong place. He thought he had reached India when he actually landed in the Americas. Thinking he was doing one thing, he was actually doing quite another. You'll have the same experience. You'll intend to do one thing and end up doing another. Sometimes it won't make any difference. Other times it may have serious consequences. So it's a good idea to get a few things straight.

First of all, you will make mistakes. No one is perfect.

Some mistakes are little oopsies that make no difference. Laugh at them and move on. But if you make a serious mistake that involves sin, you need to know that Jesus Christ died on the cross to take care of that problem. That's the second sure thing: Jesus earned forgiveness for people who sin and offers it to them. He also wants forgiven sinners to forgive themselves. When you trust in Jesus Christ who has earned forgiveness for all sin, you can face every circumstance of life— no matter what. His undeserved love is enough for you. His death on the cross for you is enough. You aren't perfect and never will be. But he was. Jesus gives his perfection to you. It covers all mistakes.

When you have made a mistake—and he has forgiven it— forget it, but not too quickly. Use it to grow. Look for the lesson each error has to teach. Make that new learning a part of your life. Resist making the same mistake again! But keep on trying. In the assurance of God's love and claiming God's forgiveness, boldly plunge forward into and through the exciting years between 12 and 20. Great things are happening. They are happening to you. Say it out loud: "Thank God I'm a teenager!"

Now let's get on to the exciting things God wants us to know as we, like the young man Jesus, "grow in wisdom and stature, and in favor with God and men." Step one? Dump some unnecessary teenage debris.

Two
DON'T BELIEVE IT

To get the most out of this book and out of your life, you need a positive self-image. You need to feel good about who you are. Do you know, and are you glad that you are a unique and wonderful person, made so by God on purpose? An enormous number of teens don't feel that way about themselves. This was reported in *Getting Along* (Minneapolis: Augsburg, 1980), a book written by Pastor Charles Mueller. The book was based on letters and notes he had received from kids all over the United States, many in response to the first edition of this book. And have you noticed the rash of articles and many studies about teenage suicide that have surfaced in the past few years? Guess what? A significant contributing cause of teenage suicide is a low self-image. Why would anyone, especially bright and bouncy teenagers, have a low self-image?

One reason many feel negative about who they are is that they have accepted distortions about themselves as facts. Young people (or their seniors) who believe the distortions, shape their view of teenagers and their responses accordingly. If you think something is true, you'll act accordingly. We need to correct some of the distortions about teenagers, and we are going to do just that. We'll make those corrections based on the *real* facts. These real facts come from a variety of reliable studies, new and old, from personal observations and experiences, and from truths gleaned from the best sources: teenagers themselves.

Dr. Jekyll and Mr. Hyde

A number of years ago a study was made among teachers concerning their view of the teenage stage. Eighty percent of those polled expressed a belief that the teen years were a period of intense emotional disturbance. More than half of the teachers felt the teen years produced a complete personality change, something like that of Dr. Jekyll and Mr. Hyde. They felt that teenagers had an excessive number of problems, that they might explode emotionally at any time, and that they were subject to severe personality maladjustments. Some teachers said that. That scares me. I believe that teachers who carry these beliefs toward teenagers will temper their actions accordingly. Do you think that a teacher who is convinced a student has a warped personality and is under the stress of intense emotional disturbance will recognize and appreciate the virtues of the student, no matter how obvious they may be?

What's doubly unfair about this is the fact that 75% of all teenagers adapt to the changes of their life with such ease that they act (and often feel) as if the tensions don't exist. In a major study of adolescence reported by *Psychology Today* it was found that "the vast majority" of early teens were trouble-free or only had problems now and then.

It is true that the teenage years are a time of significant growth, change, and adjustment in personality. But that adjustment, for most, can hardly be characterized as "a time of stress and storm" or "intense emotional disturbance." Teenagers face tough issues, perform difficult tasks, and deal with challenging decisions. True. Much of what they face is new to them and probably unexpected. Also true. That means they will have to learn how to adapt: a requirement for people of every age. And they do. Teenagers successfully confront change. They do so by using their increased intelligence, their sharpened perceptivity, and their developing social readiness to cope with difficulties. I believe they do it in a competent and generally rather matter-of-fact fashion. Let me support that with a true story.

On a January Minnesota morning, 3000 guests, half of them teens, woke up stranded by snow in a hotel. During the night an enormous snow storm had paralyzed the city, making it impossible for the hotel workers to get through. Think of it: 3000 people, half of them teens, with only the hotel's night shift skeleton crew to provide for everyone's needs. What do you *think* happened? Simply put, the kids took over. They helped in the kitchen, fed everyone, made beds, helped get luggage moved around, opened the main entrance, and had things pretty well under control by the time "help" arrived. A true story. It happened. Teens did it.

I suspect that the tragic view of teens by some teachers (and a lot of parents as well) is shaped both by a faulty memory system and our inclination to accent the negative. Too many adults don't remember how they acted when they were in their teens. They dramatize and distort what they did then and superimpose that "myth" on today's teenagers. Actually, the "sins of our youth" are not that gross or that interesting. The most noteworthy thing that can be said is that they were our first sins. Sad to say, we get better at the sinning business as we age. Our sense of shame diminishes. Our skill at dumping on people improves. We caricature the young. Sad.

That's not to say there are no troubled teenagers! There just aren't as many as some would assume. Research over the years consistently shows that only 12% to 15% of teenagers are plagued with trouble and turmoil. See? Most are not as troubled as is thought by the adults who not only don't tell it like it is, they don't even tell it like it was.

Get it straight: the vast majority of teenagers move along from challenge to challenge and from choice to choice, handling things in an acceptable, even commendable fashion. Of course, they all make mistakes. And everyone slips around on the emotional peaks and valleys. But any idea that the teen years are a period of aggravated incompetence, severe maladjustment, or uncontrollable emotional crisis, is not based on fact.

Hurry up and grow up

Another distortion is the assumption that you're supposed to grow up (whatever that means!) as quickly as possible. The sooner you become an adult, the better off you'll be. Underlining that distortion is the assumption that being an adult is better than being a teenager. The further implication is that you're supposed to act, dress, think, talk in an adult fashion. And the sooner the better. Don't you believe it.

Growing up (or what passes for that) is inevitable. The real thing happens all by itself. You can't really hurry it much. You might "act" grown up earlier than your years would indicate, but that is probably the most childish thing a person can do. Instead of being a satisfied teen, you would be applying your energies at acting like an adult—and an awkward one at that. I enjoy being what I now am. But I also enjoyed being a teenager. I don't have to give up either. I don't have to choose. Paul the apostle wrote, "I have learned to be content whatever the circumstances" (Phil. 4:11). That makes good sense. Young or old can find contentment. How? Observe the valuable things that are happening. As long as you are a teenager, act like one. Dress like a teenager. Socialize like a teenager. Take in all the experiences that surround teenagers and invite participation. Don't miss a one. You *are* a teenager. You'll be one until the last day of your 19th year. Then, later if you become a mom or dad, you will be able to encourage your son or daughter to do the same and not be afraid.

Who likes to fight?

A third distortion of life in the teens is the belief that those years are marked by constant disturbance and conflict between teens and their parents. I don't agree with that. At the very best the statement is an exaggeration.

Some young people go through intense family struggle as they work out their constantly changing relationship with their parents. That is not the same as destructive conflict. The roles in the family are changing rapidly. Young people are normally more *assertive* during these changing years as they seek to work out their proper areas of responsibility. And parents tend to hang on to their *dominance* and very reluctantly give up any real or imagined positions of control. A certain amount of awkwardness in the area of proper role relationships during the transition time, on the part of both teen and parent, can trigger times of tension. Recognize the problem. Help one another.

The reality is that the vast majority of teenagers have a positive and loving relationship with their parents and carry good feelings toward them. They don't always express those feelings as well as they could, but they have them. A 1985 study of Lutheran families surfaced an overwhelming desire of parents—and teens—to talk with each other. They want to develop, in their homes, opportunities for sharing. In the same study it was discovered that no peer has the influence of a parent, unless the parent and teen have quit trying to communicate.

One thing more: it's wonderful to discover the pleasures of treating one another as equals. There is no better time in life than when our home is filled with teenagers. You can talk about such a rich variety of subjects. Daughters and sons have much to share with parents—sometimes (but not always) more than parents have to share with them. Talk about experiences. Relax together. Learn to laugh a lot. Of course there will be flare-ups, but those are normal to life. Parents need to discover that when they are dealing with teenagers they don't always have to be right. It's OK to say, "I don't know" and ask whether one of them has the better response to the question. But mom and dad aren't always wrong, either. Everyone needs to learn how to handle one another's lack of knowledge in a way that doesn't make the others feel inadequate or unworthy.

Will parents and teens always agree? Must they? Of course not. Is it all right to argue? You better believe it. All real relationships of life have their times of agreement and times of disagreement. That's not bad; it's good. In and through arguments we explore what each of us knows and negotiate new understandings. One key thing that makes the difference between positive and helpful disagreement and destructive conflict, is the style in which the discussion is conducted.

I once ordered 500 buttons made with the message, "I could be wrong—let's talk." Then I ordered 500 more imprinted, "You may be right—let's talk." I gave those to people I cared about. Wearing one of my buttons didn't mean the wearer thought he or she was wrong or believed the other guy was right. It didn't even mean that determining who is right and who is wrong is important! It was a way of saying the wearer was willing to talk openly: I *could* be wrong and you *may* be right. And it meant the wearer believed in talk. Winston Churchill once said, "Talk, talk, talk beats fight, fight, fight." I really believe that. Each person has a part of the truth, and if anyone cuts off conversation we'll never discover the whole truth.

We can't talk with each other

The last few sentences of the previous paragraph bring us to another distortion. This one insists that there is an unbridgeable communication gap between generations. This is not so. What does exist is not a communication *gap* but a communication *difficulty* that is normal between people of different ages, of different interests, and of different experiences.

That doesn't mean people aren't able to talk with one another. But they must be conscious of communication "problems" like *intentional incomprehension* (that's when you really understand what the other person is saying but just don't want to hear it), *passive grunting* (that's a conversation with a lot of "uh huhs" and "I don't knows" that both parties know is going nowhere), and *issues defining* (that's when one party makes all the conversational rules and in the process kills any real hope of communication). Those are some illustrations of the many faces of communication gaps.

Realize it: communication is a very difficult process. You'll struggle with its many difficulties all your life. Sharing your thoughts, feelings, and ideas with another human being requires great effort and considerable skill. In that process you can stumble around over words, word meanings, word usages, and other communication difficulties until it seems you'll never get your message across. What can you do about that?

Well, don't shout at each other like frustrated tourists who think that saying an English word louder will somehow make it comprehensible to a Japanese person. You can't force meaning across a language barrier by volume, by wild gestures, and certainly not by insulting remarks. Instead of making things clearer, that kind of action aggravates, angers, and confuses. Start at another point.

Accept, in a real sense, that teenagers and their parents live in separate worlds. You are not a parent, so some things they talk about don't make sense to you. And since parents are no longer teenagers, and may have forgotten what it's like to walk in your world of daily new discovery, they may not get the message you are sending. If you can handle that, you are ready for the next step. Decide to care enough for your mom and dad to work your hardest at sharing thoughts. Resist accepting the distortion that there is an insurmountable communication gap between you and your folks. Try. Try hard. Don't let a sense of overwhelming hopelessness envelop you. Don't lose your will to try.

Barnyard morality

Another common distortion concerns the morals of young people. I really get angry when I read or hear anyone imply that the average teenager has the morals of a barnyard animal. They insinuate, or say, that teenagers are sexually permissive, easily addicted to drugs, and get drunk every weekend. That's simply not true even though those dumb Hollywood movies about teens claim the opposite. They can't be true: they are made by adults for adults.

Studies in the early 1970s revealed that at least 75% of all teenagers have well-defined moral standards and generally act on those standards with great consistency. An additional 20% have some difficulty with a healthy moral stance during the teen years but finally work their way through it. Only about 5% need help. Nearly 20 years later I think that's still true. My conviction is a far cry from the generalization that teenagers are lacking in moral integrity.

I'm not saying that there are no teenagers with low moral standards. But when you talk about the some who have moral instability you should also remember the many others who are guided by deep spiritual and moral convictions. As a matter of fact, I have come to the conclusion that the moral standard of a typical teenager is, if anything, superior to that of his or her parents. Was it teens or parents who created our X-rated age, moral laxity, and permissive society? I believe that the average teenager has a sharper sense of right and wrong, a more sensitive conscience, and a greater will to live a life reflective of Christian commitment than most people think. Don't let anyone tell you any different. And don't let anyone make you think that your Christian moral standard is an oddity, or abnormal, for someone your age. When you know your moral standards are consistent with what God requires, stick to them.

But there have been changes, and teens have been pressured by these changes. Because of that, a chapter on coping and on sexual matters has been added. There is a radical and severe change in the moral tone of our society and the moral standards which adults tolerate and encourage. Did you get it—"which *adults* tolerate"? Young people are forced by the society of their parent's creation to deal with drugs, improper sex, permissiveness of every sort, abortions, tolerated homosexuality and lesbianism, teenage alcoholism, and materialism-gone-crazy. It's tougher being a teenager today than 20 years ago. It's a dozen times tougher today than it was for those of us who made the journey nearly half a century ago. But lots of great young people make it through today's spiritual war zone with Christian flags flying. Many who at first stumbled make it too: they move into their tomorrow knowing that their red-as-crimson sin has been made whiter than snow in the blood of the Lamb.

Juvenile delinquents

Why do they always say *juvenile delinquents?* Why not use the term *adult delinquents*, or *senior-citizen delinquents?* It seems obvious to me that delinquency is as much a problem in adult life as in the teenage years. More so! So why the unfair focus?

Could it be that people are afraid of the young? Do they equate being young with being delinquent and dangerous? A television commercial, supposedly advertising the virtues of the Boy Scout movement, began with pictures of a man nervously walking down a dark street. Looking back over his shoulder he saw two shadowy figures, obviously young, moving along the sidewalk at the same speed as he. A look of relief spread over his face when, at a street light, he sees his "companions" were uniformed Boy Scouts. That may have been a good advertisement to some for a youth movement, but it seems to me it undergirds the distortion that young people are dangerous and are likely to cause harm. I don't believe that's true.

What *is* true is that in the teen years there is an inclination to do things on the spur of the moment and with great exuberance. Spontaneity and quick actions may not always be well controlled.

But that's no crime. Both are not the same as willful destructiveness. And a spontaneous experiment (even a stupid spontaneous experiment) is not the same as a commitment to a life of degenerate evil.

I don't want to say that there isn't any such thing as a juvenile delinquent. There is. Our jails prove it. There are dangerous juvenile delinquents. What they do is very serious. Many of the crimes in America today are committed by the young. Their actions are not harmless indiscretions for which they are not to be held accountable. When a badly disturbed young person does something that injures another, that action ought to be recognized for the indignity and wrong that it is. But there aren't more juvenile delinquents than there are adult delinquents. It is a sin against millions of young people to suggest that all teenagers are inclined to delinquency just because there are a few who can't control themselves and their actions.

Don't let them get you

If we can lay the cited distortions to rest we will be better able to confront serious realities that demand our attention. I don't want you to think that there are no negatives in the teenage years. Any time human beings face periods of rapid change, of human stress, and of normal difficulty, mistakes are inevitable. But teenage stress and difficulties are manageable, and, in fact, are managed quite well by teenagers. Recognize the reality but don't let distortions get you. Set them aside. Just because your father or mother went through a shattering experience doesn't mean that you will go through the same one. Or if you do have the same experience it doesn't mean you'll deal with it the same way. Daughters need not repeat the mistakes of their mothers; the same goes for sons

31

and their fathers. There is no such thing as genetic "bad blood" which makes immoral conduct predictable and inevitable.

We all sin, and all need forgiveness, but God has not only given us the forgiveness we need but the ability, through the Spirit, to change. Even when we err, when we sin—when we sin grievously—there is forgiveness for us in Christ, *and* the Spirit-empowered ability to turn our lives around. If you live down to the distorted expectations of the teenage years, it's not because there is some kind of irresistible pressure that makes you do that. Granted, satanic pressure is certainly there. But there is also a power from Christ to overcome the force of sin and be a very different and better person. By your Baptism, by the power of the Word of God, by the living presence of the Lord you can make good things happen. Let Jesus not only be the Lord *in* your life, but the Lord *of* your life.

Some of the young people with whom I share have never known (or maybe they have forgotten) the power God offers for helping people change. John 5:1-9 tells a "change" story about a man who had been unable to walk for 38 years. He had gone to the pool at Bethesda in the hope that a miracle would happen, a miracle which, in time, he had come to believe was still available to others, but not to him. But he was there. Just in case. Jesus came, looked down on the man and said, "Do you want to be healed?"

Wouldn't you think the man would have said, "Yes! Absolutely, yes! I really and truly want to be healed! And I think you can do it!" He didn't say that. Instead he began explaining his problem. He was still sick. He told Jesus there was no one to help him. Others had help, but not him. He talked about things that stood in the way of his healing. But he never answered the question.

How did Jesus handle the situation? Leaping over all the problems the man mentioned, ignoring his explanations and his excuses, Jesus went for an immediate solution. He said, "Rise, pick up your bed and walk." And the man did.

Jesus handles all distorted views the same way. As the

Lord who wants to bring a healing to you, to give you "strong legs" and great power to live your life today and in the years ahead, he asks you, "Do you want to be healed?" What's your answer?

For Jesus' sake, and for your own, say yes. Take the healing he has for you. Take it right now. Let Jesus show you who you really are . . . and whose you are. Let him tell you what he wants to do for you. You don't have to be what others say you are. You can, through him, be his kind of person. Ask him.

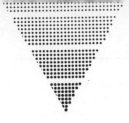

Three
MEET YOUR FAMILY

Everybody has a family. Everybody.

Sometimes a family is a houseful: five, six, or seven people. Other times it could be just three: father, mother, you. More and more often the family is two: you and your divorced mom—or dad. What if you have been adopted and share a parent with four or five stepbrothers and stepsisters? That's still a family. It also could be that both your parents are dead and your family is you and your older brother or sister. You may be living with your grandparents. Or grandma and grandpa may be living with you. Whatever its shape, that affecting/directing/nurturing/teaching/loving/fighting/caring relationship in your life that fits any of the broad membership descriptions sketched above (or others) is your family. Like fingerprints, the construction of every family is both similar and different. And there's more.

Not only who but how

The best understanding of the word *family* not only describes who is in a specific association but how the members link and how they treat each other. Some families strike you as strong and sturdy deposits of raw power just waiting to be turned on. Each person has deep attachments and intense loyalty toward every other member in the family. They always seem to know what's going on in their home and how to deal with it. Other families look so flimsy and vaporish that you feel the slightest breeze will cave in their relationship of apparently casual commitment. No one seems to take care of anyone or anything. Decisions aren't made; things just seem to happen.

Between those descriptions of extremes are other family groupings in almost infinite variety. Some are distinctively racial and nationalistic in their tone and temperament. They speak a foreign language at home and work hard at remembering the "old country," its customs, its values—even its eating habits. Others are totally Americanized and don't pay attention to any of those things. Some families can let outsiders join in without any difficulty. Others are so tightly knit that you have to be married into them for a half dozen years before you feel you have any rights at all. With some families those old customs, often generations old, add a dimension to the family life of only one wing of a clan, while another part of the same family moves on, leaving the past behind them.

And what about the variety of relationships within the family? How do parents (individually and collectively) relate to children, children to each other, and children to parents? That kind of relating can be powerful. I remember a little girl I tried to teach the Lord's Prayer. She just couldn't learn it. Other things she memorized with ease, but the Lord's Prayer was a stumbling block. When I finally got smart enough to ask her why it was so difficult she said, "The Lord's Prayer makes me hate God." Then she told me about her own father. He regularly got drunk, beat her mother and the children, and would then go roaring out into the night smashing things as he went. As far as she was concerned any prayer that started out, "Our Father" could only be bad news, and any God who had the name *Father* was sure trouble. She hoped and prayed that God wasn't like a father—not her father, anyway. See how family can affect you?

Each family is different in its own way. Sometimes the differences are subtle, and sometimes they hit you like a ton of bricks. These differences of individuals and of combinations of individuals are part of the uniqueness of any family. To help you better understand what's going on in your family (or reinforce the understanding you already have), I want to share several insights into family living. I believe they will help you evaluate more accurately what's going on in your own home, including why and how things happen as they do.

My first club

Many sociologists call the family "the primary organization of human life." I don't always understand everything sociologists say, but that description helped me understand some of the things about my family and my life.

My first club! I've joined many clubs since I first became a "family" man, but that first club stands out as exceptional for many reasons. For example, unlike other clubs I've joined since, I can't resign from this club (my family), or erase the experiences (good and bad) this club has brought to me. Those experiences are with me every day. As a matter of fact, everything I have ever done in my life is in some way related to what I was taught (or was not taught) and what I learned (or should have learned) in my first club—my family.

It was in my first club, my family, that I learned how to relate to other people. They taught me how to live happily with others. They gave me the skills I would need: how and when to compromise, the art of cooperation, and ways to express basic concern. I had my earliest lessons in love (both in what love should be and in what love shouldn't be) from my family. What I now reflect as a father and a husband was shaped in my family association of long ago. It was there I was first taught my responsibility toward others and could test my understanding of it. I developed basic abilities at bargaining, arguing, persuading, and encouraging. I spent more hours learning important things for life in the context of my family than I've spent in all the other classrooms of my life. You, too, I'm sure! All the other formal or informal organizations I join the rest of my life, combined, will never be as important, or have as great an effect on me as my family. The sociologists are right. The family is the primary organization of my life, my first and my most important club.

We do our thing—our way

Without ever actually meeting your family, I can say without hesitation that it does its family thing in its own way. Everything that happens in your family, from the way your mother relates to your father, to how they, together, relate to you (and other members of the family), plus all the other exciting things that take place in your home, are at least somewhat different from the way things happen in any other family. On the surface your family may seem similar, or even almost identical, to other families, but there are always differences. Some are subtle. Others are dramatic.

You will most clearly understand what I'm saying if you get married and you and your spouse begin meshing your family experiences together as you shape your new family unit. That's when you will realize how many differences there can be between families. How will you decide which one will take care of the checkbook? You'll fall back on how it was done in your family. What if in one of your families the mother paid bills, and in the other the father? Which is right? And you'll have to decide when you open your Christmas gifts. Was it on Christmas Eve in one family and Christmas morning in the other? Did one always have dinner (or was it called supper?) at 6:30 and the other at 5:00? And then come those questions about what kind of stuffing to put in the Thanksgiving turkey (oyster or raisin), who washes dishes (everyone or just the

37

girls), what kind of sicknesses require a trip to the doctor (every little scratch or nothing short of a broken leg). Those are a few illustrations of differences in family practice. Those differences are very significant. You will have lots of fun sorting them out. But what will make the most difference is working out your approach to the way your families made decisions.

Family decision making

The Latin origin of the word *decide* means "to cut." It's like when you lay out a pattern on wood or cloth, pause to make sure everything is right, and then make that first cut. Once the saw—or the scissors—goes to work, things are changed, usually permanently. Decisions are "cuts." They change things, sometimes permanently. That's point one: decisions change things. The second point is just as simple and true: how you make a decision can be as important, maybe more important, than the decision you make. Some families make decisions in a very direct and uncluttered fashion; get dad on your side, and if he agrees with you it's all downhill from there. Every decision is finally made by him. Is that the way your family works? That doesn't sound like a very good way to do things. How can others learn if only one person always decides? Other families gather around the table and then, as a group, discuss and negotiate until common consent develops. In other families, decisions are made by going ahead and doing what you want to do until someone stops you.

Later in this book we'll share more about how to make decisions in the family and elsewhere. But for now realize that decisions do get made in your family. Before you announce a conviction that everyone in the world does decision making your way (or at least ought to), take a good look at how you finally resolve the many questions that arise as a part of family living. Then investigate and compare how other families do the same thing. Are all processes alike, even identical? Are they different? Look very carefully. Make some decisions about deciding. When you understand how decisions are made in your family, you will be in a better position to eventually work out the kind of decision-making style you want for your future. Most people like an inclusive style—one that involves others. It spreads the responsibility. However, any good process is acceptable if it resolves the problem and brings peace and happiness in the home.

Families have boundaries

There came a time in the Old West when cattlemen began stringing barbed wire around their ranches. That spiky wire let everyone know whose land was whose, and kept the cattle where they belonged. The barbed wire that kept cattle in also kept uninvited strangers and rustlers out. Simply put, the barbed wire *boundaried*.

Every family has boundaries and, just as true, every family sets boundaries. These boundaries establish and define what it means when a family says "we." They determine who is a family member for whom you are responsible and on whom you can depend for support in a time of need.

For some families their "we" describes a very tight-knit little group. It is limited to those who actually live in the family home. Everyone else in the whole world is an outsider—and stays that way until the family decides differently. Others may stretch "we" to include a few relatives, and occasionally a close friend of the family. (Were you ever taught to call some unrelated family friend "Uncle Fred" or "Cousin Ruth"?) Some families are so loose boundaried that they include anyone who wants to join them. What's it like in your family?

Yours may be a tightly-boundaried family or a loosely-boundaried family, but it is boundaried. How can you tell? Look around. Does everyone have to eat together? Are prayers said together before every meal? Do you have to tell your parents exactly where you are going to be when you go out in the evening? The answers to those questions are your boundaries. Where you put those kinds of boundaries is what makes your family different. Let's take a closer look. We'll start with tightly boundaried families.

Tightly boundaried families emphasize taking care of their own without outside interference or assistance. Remember the Hatfields and the McCoys? Tightly boundaried families provide security and safety. But they have problems. One problem is that when the boundaries are too snug, members feel choked and are unable to relate adequately to the rest of the world. A dangerous example of this is one of the world's most famous tightly boundaried families: the Mafia. They are exclusive in the extreme.

On the other hand, families with loose boundaries, or almost undiscernable boundaries, have problems, too. They have no screening standards by which members of the family can evaluate friends, establish values, or make decisions. Some loosely boundaried families (more and more common today) really have no standards at all. Everyone does what they want. Only if people start bumping against others (and no one is quite sure who the others are) are any questions asked. Loosely boundaried families are guided by whatever fad is in fashion at that moment, or by individual whim, or by nothing. Stories about loosely boundaried families have a way of popping up in the newspapers. When you read about them they are usually in trouble.

The family style with the greatest growth potential for all its members is one which maintains an intentional balance between loose boundaries and tight boundaries. This healthiest family has within itself the capacity for openness, and yet it also has a solidness. It recognizes that its greatest influence on other members is through example rather than by control. In such a family it's possible to introduce new ideas, adopt new approaches, offer new information, and even suggest the acceptance of new people. In the face of the new this family reviews whatever is brought before it, discusses it, and finally makes an evaluation to see whether it meets the family standard. If the new thing measures up, it is in. If not, it is out.

Another name for "family standard" is "rules." While all families have some rules (even if their rules are that they have no rules), well-boundaried families have good rules. That means they start with God's rules.

We have rules here

After leading the descendants of Jacob out of Egypt to the promised land, one of the first things God did was to set down rules for how they should live with God and with others. These rules are summarized in the Ten Commandments. Actually there were many more rules than 10. You will find some of them in Exodus, Leviticus, Numbers, and Deuteronomy. The purpose of the rules was to govern the life-style of that huge "family" known as the children of Israel. You could tell who belonged to the family by noting who accepted the rules and tried hard to keep them. They were like a family. Consciously or unconsciously, every boundaried family adopts rules for determining acceptable and unacceptable behavior for family members and for others. Family rules are very seldom written down. Family members know them, or soon learn what they are. Examples? Easy.

One family I know has a rule that whenever questions of importance come up for discussion, the family always sits down, talks it over, and then the mother makes a binding decision. Other families have rules about how the family eats and who eats with whom. One family I know has a rule that the children and the mother eat at one time, and the father always eats at another. Some families have rules that money earned by any member of the family is to be brought home, turned over to the father, and then shared, as he determines, with the one who has the greatest need. Families have rules about attendance at church and Sunday school, rules about dating, rules about friends, rules about clothing, rules about household duties.

Many families have rules that are extremely important to

them and are never broken. I know of a family that is not very religious, and yet it has a rule that on Mother's Day everyone goes to church together, and that rule cannot be broken. Other rules may get bent quite often, but not that one! In our house we have a rule that everyone should make their beds before going to school, but it doesn't always work out that way. That rule may be up for change soon.

One more thing: your family's major rule may be another family's minor rule. If you get confused and ignore a major rule, thinking it's a minor rule, all kinds of unpleasant things take place. Great family stories revolve about that problem.

Rules are important

Whether rules are useful and sensible, whether they last a long time, whether they are strange and maybe even harmful, the important thing to understand is that rules are vital for family living. They help the family be a family. Why? Go back to where we began: boundaries. Rules help set the boundaries of family membership. Those who know and keep the rules are members of the family. Those who don't know or who won't keep a family's rules may find their membership in jeopardy. Rules help us develop a sense of "we-ness" that stays with us throughout life.

One more important thing about rules: they bring order and predictability to a situation that might otherwise be chaotic and confusing. For example, a rule that says you must be home by 11:00 P.M. may cramp your style, but it also guarantees that there won't be a family hassle when you come home—as long as you beat the deadline. Wouldn't it be terrible if you never knew when you were supposed to walk through the front door? Every night there would be a fight.

Furthermore, if you obey the rules of your family you know that others in the family are obeying them as well. This assures you that if you are to wash dishes on Mondays, Wednesdays, and Fridays, you can plan to go out after dinner on Tuesdays, Thursdays, and Saturdays because you know your brother or sister, who take the alternate days, are bound by the same rules as you. Or, if your family has the rule that all your parents expect from you at school is to try very hard, without regard to grades, you don't have to worry about a C minus in geometry—if everyone else knows that you've been making a genuine effort.

Finally, family rules can help you out of some very sticky situations. Have you ever been asked to do something you really didn't want to do, or perhaps didn't think you ought to, but you didn't know how to get out of it? You probably said instead, "I'd really like to, but my folks won't let me." By "folks" you meant the family rules.

Don't knock rules. At least don't knock them until you've come to learn what the rules are and have developed an appreciation for some of their values.

We have rules about rules

As if having rules isn't enough, all families also have rules about rules. They have rules about how the rules can be changed and when there is an exception to the rule. One family has a rule that whoever gets to the television set first chooses the program and no one has the right to change the channel. But here comes the rule about the rule: While no one can change the channel selected by the first person who got there, whenever dad comes into the room he can watch any program he wants. Or maybe your family has a rule that everyone must help clear the table after dinner except the one who has a babysitting job that evening. That's a rule about rules.

One important rule about rules is the family's rule about how the rules can be changed. Rules must (and do) get changed quite regularly. They change because a family's life situation is constantly changing. If the rules don't change, growth within the family can't take place. Actually, out-of-date rules are not helpful. They are unreasonably repressive. The process by which rules are changed is an intricate process called *renegotiation*.

If there is to be peace in the family during the process of rule changing, it's important that everyone (especially you) knows not only that change can happen and how it happens, but, most important, why it happens. Out of the "why" grows the basis for renegotiation. The "why" of renegotiation is directly related to something that has been taking place in you, and indirectly in your family, from the day you were born. Since your birth you have been moving through two phases of your life, and now, as a teenager, you are moving well along toward a third. After we consider these three changes, we will come back to renegotiation.

From dependence . . .

The first phase of your life is one of dependence. You were born totally dependent. Someone else had to feed you, burp you, diaper you, bundle you up, and keep you warm. Everything you needed for life was done by others. You could do nothing. Then someone taught you how to speak, to walk, to take minimal care of yourself. Little by little you learned how to feed yourself without sticking a spoon in your nose. Your total dependence gave way to a second stage of your life.

. . . To interdependence . . .

Interdependence describes that phase of your life in which you not only received but also gave. In this phase, one that has covered most of your existence up to now, you got help from others, but you also gave help to others. For instance, your father may have taught you how to throw a ball. When your brother came along your father was much busier than when you were a child. It fell to you to teach your brother how to throw a ball. That's interdependence. You received and now you give.

Or, as a child, you might have seen the lawn only as a

place to play. You used it. You did nothing to it or for it. As you grew older you started to do a little weeding, some clipping, and finally were given full responsibility for the lawn. In the passage of time there develops a growing balance between what you need to have others do for you, and what you do for others. Hasn't it been steadily tilting in favor of helping others, more and more, with every passing year? It's not strange to me that somewhere in the teen years you develop a desire for a third phase. You move to that phase in the late teens, a phase called independence.

. . . To independence

With every passing year you yearn more and more for independence. It never arrives in an absolute sense (as if you don't need anyone else to help you), but it does come in a sense that you feel free to do with your life what you wish. It is strange, yet true, that when the possibility of the independence draws near, most of us reassert the need for interdependence. We go looking for a mate, or long to spend more time at home. We never become fully independent, but the vision of independence in this world always hangs out there waiting for our embrace. Occasional yearnings for independence are a sign that your family is not going to last forever in the form you have known it. You are sensing—maybe even seeking—something else.

Renegotiation

During all the years in which you are moving from dependence, to interdependence, toward independence, things are changing in your world. You are changing. All the members of your family are changing. Your family situation is changing. Even the laws of the land are changing. As people change, and as the context in which they live changes, the rules change too. That process of changing family rules to meet changing circumstances is either explosive revolution (not good) or God-pleasing renegotiation. I urge renegotiation. It works. It always has. Remember?

Think about when you were a little child. On sunny days didn't your mother put you out in the fenced backyard to play? You liked to play there. It was fun in the backyard. But you discovered your home had a front yard, too. You wanted to play there. In time you made it from the backyard to the front. How did you get from the backyard to the front yard? Renegotiation. You renegotiated the rule which said that whenever you wanted to play outside you must play in the backyard. I'm guessing the way you renegotiated was to plead, beg, cajole, and maybe cry. Did your mother make you promise you would never step one inch over the sidewalk, or pass the bordering driveway that marked the boundaries of your family property? And did you promise? You bet! It was great to play in the front yard! You escaped from the backyard to play in the front yard through renegotiation. Rules were changed. But there is more to this story, right?

One day, while you were playing in the front yard, you noticed a little boy or girl across the street playing in his or her front yard. Even if you didn't know the word, in your mind you realized it was time to renegotiate. So you pestered, pleaded, begged, and maybe cried again, until you got to cross the street. Once again rules were changed and new ones took their place. And the promises! You had to take a great oath that you would go only to your friend's house, and nowhere else, and that you would always tell your mother when you were going. Renegotiation!

With the passing of the years your boundaries got stretched more and more. Through renegotiation you expanded the number of places to which you could go, how long you could stay there, when you had to return, with whom you might play, what you could do, and countless other things. Every change in those rules was marked by a process of renegotiation. Sometimes it was simple, and sometimes it was complicated. But there was always a change of past patterns of acceptable activity. And it always meant greater freedom.

The toughest renegotiation

The toughest kinds of renegotiation take place during your teenage years. You're not only moving from early teens to middle teens to late teens (Chapter 1), but you're also moving around in the world of interdependence toward what you now see as the goal of independence. What's more, the changes taking place within yourself are happening so swiftly, and so unpredictably, that you hardly know from day to day what you want to do. You may yearn to be freed from your family so you can find your own identity, yet you have this funny sensation that makes you like the family and the security, love, and support (and family car) which it represents. In addition, your world is expanding, your environment is transforming, your circle of friends is changing, you have new social goals— and all these things are happening at once, and superfast. Through it all you have an accelerating desire to change the old rules so that you can try something new. But as long as you are in the family, any time the rules get changed you'll have to renegotiate.

I can't say enough about the speed with which things are changing in your teenage life. A father asked me to help in his family renegotiation process. He really didn't know that term, but he did realize that he was having a lot of trouble with his daughter and that some kind of change was needed. He was thrilled in early March when he and his daughter seemed to agree on acceptable conduct on the part of both. In late June he was terribly angry because his daughter wanted to rediscuss the agreements they had made in March. He thought she was unfair. The truth is that things had changed. Really. And she had changed. Fundamentally. But it was tough on him.

You may think an agreement you renegotiated a month

ago is already ready for renegotiation—while mom and dad are only now starting to adjust to what they agreed to then. It's hard on your parents to renegotiate constantly. Their world doesn't change that fast. They may think that "the-matter-is-finally-settled" at the same time you are getting ready for the new debate! But try to understand how your parents feel. Maybe it's not as important for them to understand why you have the urge to renegotiate as it is for you to understand how tough it is on them. Let me encourage you to keep the process of renegotiation going in a loving way. Bargain away, but as you bargain, make sure your renegotiation helps build the family, not destroy it.

Come on now, be fair

Bargaining that builds the family is "fair bargaining." For instance, if you are just playing games renegotiating for something you really don't want or for something you think your parents won't or couldn't give to you anyway, you are not engaged in fair bargaining. You aren't renegotiating honestly. Sound far-fetched? That's exactly what you are doing when you tell your parents you want to go out with a guy (or a girl) who you know is far too old for you, hoping that your parents won't let you do it. When you keep trying to renegotiate with them on this subject, knowing how they feel (and how you really feel), you are not being fair.

It's also not fair to start renegotiating with your parents and then, right in the middle of the process, give up the whole request without ever having really made your request clear. That leaves your parents confused, unable to make a reasonable response to your desire. They don't know what you want—or why. It is your responsibility to make your request clear and to give them an understanding of what you wish. An abrupt "forget it" or a vague "it's nothing" makes life unnecessarily tough.

It's also not fair to renegotiate when you know your parents can't handle the matter emotionally, financially, or legally.

Don't ask them to let you drive the car when you're under age. Don't try to get a phone in your room if your parents don't have the money. Don't ask them to lie about your age. Renegotiation always implies a responsible reasonableness on your part. At least be as reasonable as you know how.

Good renegotiation takes into consideration what everyone must give up if one person's desires are fulfilled. Every time you renegotiate, things change not only for you but for at least one other person—usually many more. Be aware of that. Remember, too, that pouting, slamming doors, angry or emotional words, impenetrable silence—all get in the way of successful renegotiation. You may finally get your way by using those means, but the price you pay with this abuse of the family is higher than any victory is worth.

Instead, whenever you come to negotiate, use that "mind-expansion" that we discussed in Chapter 1. Try a little logic. Develop a deeper understanding of others. Start operating on both sides of the table. Ask yourself questions like, "Why does dad feel like he does about the dance?" It may be that he can't afford the dress you'd like to have for the dance. If you try to understand him, you may discover that renegotiation happens much more easily. Maybe you can help him change. Or, if you're in a renegotiation process with a little sister who has always caused you grief, it may pay to wonder out loud, "Could my sister act so hateful under stress toward me because she thinks it's the only way she can get my attention, the attention she wants, and needs?" Always renegotiate your relationships from the position of your new-found teenage insights.

Open your eyes, look around, keep the renegotiation process in motion, be reasonable, and let love lead you. If those are your inner feelings, I'm confident you'll never be far from fair.

Meet your family

With some of these things in mind, isn't now a great time to "meet" your family? I once read that every law of nature could be easily observed in anyone's backyard. Is it possible that all the intricacies of the universe lie exposed just outside your back door? I believe so. And I believe, in the same way, every useful lesson of society and every strengthening discovery of life is tucked away somewhere within your own family. Discover those things through and with your unique family. Check out your family boundaries. Ponder its rules. Review the process of renegotiation. Build your tomorrow, for you will be tomorrow what you are becoming today.

And not least, remember the family is God's idea. Psalm 68:6 says, "God sets the lonely in families. . . ." That means God decided that people shouldn't be left alone to wander about by themselves, but that they should have the reinforcement of brothers, sisters, mothers, fathers, aunts, uncles, and grandparents—just to name a few. God surrounds you with all that you need for support, security, reinforcement, care, and most of all, love. It's all there waiting for you. Reach out for it. Help develop it. God wants you to have it. Meet your family!

Four

LEARN TO TRUST YOURSELF

The world-famous psychologist, Erik Erikson, said that one of the first tasks any human being must accomplish in life is to claim for themselves a sense of personal trust. Based on the letters I received from teenagers, Dr. Erikson is absolutely right! The chapter chosen by teenagers for "most important to you" was this one, Chapter 4. Most teenagers who wrote didn't realize how much they missed self-trust—until they learned how to claim it. So hang on! You're going to gain a lot in the next few pages. Start with this: most of us have trouble trusting ourselves.

There are many reasons self-trust is so highly prized and so seldom recognized by oneself. Some teens begin with a very low estimate of their worth. Others have little confidence in their ability. It's almost as if they enjoy their low self-esteem and the constant put-downs they experience. They are like Groucho Marx who, when he was once asked to join a club, declined, saying, "I refuse to join a club that would have a man like me as a member!"

I don't want to twist Groucho's remark. He is a comedian

and comedians often make themselves the butt of their own jokes. He may or may not have been serious in his self-evaluation. But he could have been. If so, he certainly represents the self-view of many teenagers! Regardless of his seriousness, there's a vast difference between his comment and the heroine's attitude in the musical, "The Unsinkable Molly Brown." At one point in that Broadway show, she belts out a triumphant song, almost shouting, "I believe in me!" Without knowing one single additional word of those lyrics, you understand its message. "I believe in me!" breathes trust, confidence, assurance, and a positive self-image. Want to feel that way about yourself? Why not?

What is your self-image? Is it positive? Is it negative? Does your self-image say to others that you have a healthy appreciation of who you are? Or does it say, "I don't trust me . . . and I don't think you ought to trust me either"? Do you come on like a groveling Groucho Marx? Or an emphatic Molly Brown? Let's see. Answer a few questions to test your level of self-trust. Give the questions a yes or no.

▶ Have you ever decided to try out for some kind of team and then changed your mind because you didn't think you were good enough for it—and were afraid to find out?

▶ Have you ever sat silently in your seat at school, declining to volunteer to do something you'd like to do, for fear that your might fail or make a fool of yourself?

▶ Have you ever avoided speaking in public because you thought people would laugh at your thoughts and the way you would express them, even though you believed them quite good?

▶ Have you ever wished you were someone else? I don't mean a day-dreamy kind of romantic hope, but a beat-to-the-ground, desperate yearning to escape your perceived personal flaws.

I suspect you've answered yes to all four. I did as a teenager, and, because no one told me I could be different, I felt that way about myself well into my post-21 years. After I intentionally (I mean I did it to myself—no one else did!) let opportunities get by, I wanted to just kick myself. I realized that I could have done just as well as the person who was finally chosen. Other times, I now realize, if I had made the effort I could have learned to do the thing I wanted to do very well, even though at first I might have been rather average. I am sure I have always been good enough to play on the team some time, or get a bit-part in the play, or maybe at least introduce someone who could speak much clearer than I. But I just sat there, glued to my chair, with my head down.

Most people really don't know what they can do or what they can't do. They don't know because they haven't tried. The reason they haven't tried is because they don't trust themselves. It's just that simple.

For the moment forget about "most people." Focus on you. Reread the previous paragraph, only substitute your name for all those "most peoples" and "theys." Then work through the next three serious—very serious—questions: (1) Do you know what trust means? (2) Do you know what exciting doors open when the first faint glimmer of self-trust shows up in your life? (3) Will you trust me as I write for you about trusting yourself?

What does trust mean?

The dictionary says trust is "assurance of one's integrity," "veracity," and "assured anticipation." Does that make things clearer? Not to me! Such a definition may help somebody, but not me. Let's look for help elsewhere. The Bible?

The Bible words translated as *trust* most often mean, "to lean on." When you trust something, you can and do lean on it. Trust a wall and you lean back against it unafraid that it will collapse. If you trust a chair, you settle down in it. When you trust a plate glass window, you slouch against it without fear. The Bible definition looks good: when you trust something you lean on it, and when you lean on something you trust it. It's the same way when you trust yourself. When you trust yourself you lean on your abilities, rely on your judgment, and are confident in your belief that you can do something. And you know what? Things start happening! I can mention four things that will happen for sure!

1. You will experience new adventures. When you trust yourself, you discover that you can move into new areas of experience. When Columbus trusted himself and his judgment that the world was round, he started raising money to buy ships. Once the money was raised through his persuasive and infectious confidence he cast off from Europe and led those three vessels across the Atlantic. It all happened because he trusted himself. Something like this will happen in your life— when you trust yourself. New adventures will simply leap at you. Don't ask me what they'll be. I don't know. But they come. They always come to the bold and confident.

2. You will develop a positive self-image. When trust enters your life, your attitude about yourself changes. You will experience a growing confidence in what you can do. You will accept new opportunities. Do you remember your first fearful trip up the steps of the slippery slide? I've watched children kicking and screaming as their parents take them to the top and send them scooting down. Not long after that first fearful adventure, the same child is shouting, "Watch me! Watch me!" as he actually runs up those same steps to the top. But we're not talking about what may seem a never-never land. A quick check will show that you have already built a positive self-image of yourself in many areas. They may not seem important, but they all imply trust. You climb trees. Or at least you could if you wanted to. You walk to school by yourself. You read out loud before the class. Maybe you have asked someone for a date—or agreed to go on one. There was a time when you couldn't, or wouldn't do any of those things (probably more wouldn't than couldn't). Why do you do at least some of those things now? Easy answer: you have a positive self-image in those particular areas. In some of those areas (or others like them) you have confidence that you can do something. Why? Because you already selectively trust yourself.

3. Jealousy of others will disappear. After you've learned to trust yourself, you discover that you can also rejoice in the accomplishments of others. You no longer feel you have to comment about the success of another, "Oh—that's nothing!" You are happy to see others star in areas of their interest and ability. You'll like yourself better after you have conquered that "green-eyed monster" called jealousy. And more. Others will like you better too. Jealousy evaporates as trust develops.

4. You will polish your capacity to improve. Somewhere along the line, like everyone else, you will begin to identify your personal limits. You can't do everything. And here's the good news: you don't even have to try. Instead of ranging all over, you can begin finding the borders of your ability in order to determine whether those borders are immovable boundaries that won't budge, or temporary fences ready to be pushed back. If you find they are like concrete walls, trust yourself and move on to another area. It took me six years of piano lessons to learn that I can't play very well. I'll never improve. I lack the proper hand/eye coordination. But I don't worry about it. I still plunk away privately for my own satisfaction, and I cheer the musical ability of others. I make a great audience. Every artist needs one. As for myself, I exert my highest concentration on those areas in which I have abilities. I strive to strengthen them while looking for interesting new things to do every day. I can hardly wait to try the new things that keep popping up. Since I first wrote these paragraphs I have learned how to whistle, draw a recognizable face, write a TV script, grow beautiful roses, travel in Brazil, and so many other new adventures. It all happened through an improving self-trust.

How trust works

To show you how this works I offer two examples, one from a moment in my life, the other an experience that touched the life of another.

I still remember that grim day toward the end of my high school years when I sat down and asked, "Isn't there something that I can do better than anyone else I know?" You'd think that in my little circle of friends I would excel somewhere. But I didn't. After I looked it all over I had to say, "There's nothing I can do better than someone else I know." How depressing! I wasn't the best in anything. I was good enough to play baseball on the school team, but I was never first string. I could sing in the choir, but I was not qualified for the quartet. I was a perpetual quarter finalist. I was good enough to get a chance at track, speech, debate, honor roll, and student government, but I was never in the finals. My grades were average. My physical ability was average. My capacity to motivate others was average. My singing was average. I concluded that I was average. I was just all-around-average, and I felt badly.

It took me a few years to discover that very few people are all-around-average. Most people excel in one thing or another, while failing miserably in most other areas. I didn't excel anywhere. But I didn't really fail anywhere either. As an all-around-average guy I hacked away at about anything, confident of doing at least a passable job. Maybe someone else had to put the final touches on what I began, but I had great fun doing my limited thing.

I still fit that description rather well and I have learned to like it. It keeps me in touch with the common people who know a lot more about failing, and averageness, than about being the star. It allows me to understand something of the experience of this world's achievers. Through it all I've come to trust my "average" self. I may not get every job done, but I can move any job far enough along so that success is inevitable in the hands of others. I'm a part of the team. I'm an important part. And I like it. I trust myself for what I am. I trust others.

I know of another boy who just couldn't make it in a classroom. He failed about everything there was to fail. He wasn't a student and he knew it. So did everyone else. But could he ever whittle wood into figures! Very few people, he discovered, could whittle as well as he. He decided to focus on whittling and began carving all kinds of intricate wooden figures. He pushed the whittling boundary as far as he could and was amazed to see what he could do. Today he makes a good living selling his wood carvings. He has, over the years, developed a healthy sense of trust in himself, within the boundaries of his ability. There aren't many people who look down on him. More important, he doesn't look down on himself.

Trust yourself. Lean on yourself. Try things—even everything. Go ahead. The teenage years stretch out before you as a grand time to find out what you can do. Don't be afraid of failure. God made you something very special. Find out what that special thing is. God put that specialness in you. You won't be disappointed in the gift he gave. Find out who you really are. Find out by trusting and leaning on yourself.

Responsibility

One of the most beautiful words in the English language (but for some people grim and distasteful) is the word *responsibility*. Would you believe that people who trust themselves go looking for responsibility? They go looking for responsibility because they have confidence in what they can do. The basketball player who thinks he can make the shot yells for the ball at the crucial moment of the game. The girl who knows she can dance wants to get out on the floor and exhibit her skills. The couple who believe they can be good parents try to have children. Seeking and accepting responsibility is fun. It produces inner joy. Responsible people like to say, "I decided to do this!"

When you trust yourself you go looking for responsibility. For example, when you trust your good taste, you don't ask your mother to go shopping with you. You want to go by yourself. When you trust your ability to recognize a bargain, you spend your money with confidence and you're happy to show your friends or parents what a good buy you made. Responsible people want to do challenging new things. They enjoy doing them.

When you start trusting yourself you almost automatically search for areas of responsibility. And taking on more responsibility means you will have more and more fun, more and more satisfaction, more and more confidence in yourself, and a deepening awareness of your own personness. It all builds. But you must start.

What about self-centeredness?

It is possible that trusting yourself may make you self-centered, but that is not likely to happen. Seeking for responsibility is the opposite of being egotistical or self-centered. Self-centered people don't trust themselves. They actually avoid responsibility because any failure would injure, even crush, their warped self-image. All their energies are expended on taking care of and idolizing their own little me while chopping away at the accomplishments of others. Self-centered people keep bringing up their virtues (even though they are afraid to test them in a crisis) so that others may stand in admiration. But a person who trusts himself comes at life from a very different perspective. You will know the difference.

If you think you are too self-centered you can do something about it. You don't have to stay that way. You can change. God will help you change. God will turn you around, if you ask. God will give you a new mind. God promises both of those things through repentance. God will expand your world and open your eyes so you can see the important things around you. Then you won't have to spend your time preoccupied with taking care of yourself. God will teach you how to handle failure. If you fail here and there in the process of growing (everyone does), God will show you what forgiveness means. God will help you forget your mistakes and get on with life in the same way that all our sins are forgotten in Christ Jesus.

Trust helps in other ways

I don't want you to think that trusting will give you only the few things I've mentioned so far. You will be able to do many more things. Let me list two for starters.

1. You will be able to let others know you care about them. Trusting yourself helps you take the risks of love and concern for others by expressing your feelings clearly. Words of love and actions of concern tell everyone that even when the going gets tough you will be their friend. They can depend on you. When you trust yourself enough to care about others, you are free to tell others in many different ways that you are interested in what happens to them. That builds relationships, strengthens families, reinforces marriages. One question thousands of teens asked me over the years is, "Why can't my mom (or dad) say I love you to me?" A companion is, "Why can't my folks ever compliment me and tell me I did a good job?" I would guess many parents are silent because they don't trust their parenting skills or are afraid you will laugh at their love. And I'm guessing further that they are reluctant to compliment for fear you might later fail and make them look bad. Dumb reasoning? I think so. They need to learn to trust themselves. Trusting yourself helps. Period.

2. You will be able to share your inner feelings with others, and others will share their feelings with you. Don't you tell the people you trust all kinds of personal things? But you are careful with people you don't trust. They may laugh. The reason you lay bare your soul with some is because you are able to talk about yourself (that means you trust yourself) and you are able to pass that sense of trust on to them (and so you tell them). People who don't trust themselves don't trust others

either. When you trust, you share inner feelings. Pretty simple, huh?

How do I learn to trust?

How do I learn to trust? Where do I start?

Starting isn't very complicated. Trust breeds trust, which breeds trust, which breeds trust, and so on. In order to trust you have to trust. It therefore looks to me that the first move toward learning how to trust is to dive in. Look around for the clearest signs of some personal ability and make your plunge there. Start checking out your potential areas for building trust by doing something that may seem strange: talk to yourself. That's right. Sit down and have an out-loud chat with yourself. In that conversation explore what you think makes you tick, the gifts and skills that may be packed inside. Identify as many areas with possibilities as you can. Write them down. Who knows more about you than you do? See what you come up with.

If you aren't so sure that your answers are right, isolate a few likely areas and test your answers with someone who seems to have a good track record for trustworthiness. Your parents? The counselor at school? A sister? Your pastor? Friend? One or the other will take you seriously and give you an opinion on your opinion about you. Then you can start by building on what you find.

Test your congruence

During that talk about yourself test your congruence. That's right: *congruence*. You may have bumped into that word in geometry. Two shapes are said to be congruent when you can place one on top of the other and they match perfectly. In terms of our concern of the moment, congruence means that you can match the inside-you to the outside-you. They fit, one on top of the other. Perfectly. Or reasonably so. There is an inside-you (all of us keep it disguised much of the time) and there is an outside-you (one everyone can see). When those two match, you are a congruent person.

Check your congruence. Look at your actions. Do these outside expressions match your inside feelings? If they do, you are congruent. That's good. If they don't, oops! You are then probably spending much of your time hiding the one—or masking the other. The more time you spend trying to make your incongruent self look congruent, the less time you can spend reaching out toward others. Congruent people have the will, and a way, of getting close to others, especially other congruent people. They don't waste time hiding things. Is that you? I hope so. If it isn't, try to get those two parts of you lined up. Make up your mind to match the inside-you and the outside-you. If you do you'll be ready for this: you will be able to deal with the potentially threatening reality that you are different from other people. That's not bad. It just reflects the way God put you together.

People are different

When a person first discovers he or she is different it can be threatening. The first impulse is to change quickly to become like everyone else. Before you make any radical change in your life trying to be like someone else, do some thinking about *difference*. Let's do a little right now.

Is it true that you have to give up your preference for classical music just because everyone else seems to like hard rock? Is something wrong with you because you don't like to play baseball? Must you be ashamed to discover that you really don't want to go to the kind of parties most other people seem to enjoy? My answer is no. In and of themselves these are only indicators that you are different. And you are. Accept that.

You will find that the positive actions of others may change you, or yours may change others. That will happen. Change is all right. But change shouldn't come from pressure either on you or from you. Let it happen naturally in its own time. And if change doesn't happen, that can be all right too. A person who knows and trusts himself or herself can be happy being different in a variety of areas. For that person it will also be all right for other people to be different, as well. More than that, when you trust yourself you can actually treasure and rejoice in the differences that exist. Which leads us a little deeper into the question of difference: the contexts in which you live.

Context is important

Context refers to all that surrounds us and affects how we act. Our *people-context,* for instance, includes ourselves, our family, and our friends. All those people have direct effect on us.

Other "contexts" also include God, our social circumstances, the accepted customs of our time. Part of our context is certain realizations, like recognizing that nothing is appropriate all the time, or everywhere. Example? A swimsuit is great on the beach, but not so good in a snowstorm. An abrupt order like, "get out of here!" may be the right thing to say when the house is on fire, but it causes trouble if blurted out at a party. Where you are, with whom you are, what you are doing, your level of self-trust, your congruence, and lots of other things, together, make up your context.

You need to be aware of your context at all times so that you can act appropriately within the context in which you find yourself. You may bumble around at first as you try to work with context, but as time goes on you will learn to sense where you are. A funny joke based on national origin may be hilarious and appropriate among your friends, but may be in poor taste when told in the company of the wrong group. Wearing the right clothes is a matter of context: blue jeans for a barbeque and a tux as best man at a wedding. If you make a mistake that is offensive or disturbing because you didn't understand the context, don't be reluctant to apologize. Honest apologies are part of developing a sense of trustworthiness and practicing congruence. Shape the things you do to the context in which you find yourself, and to the trust level with which you hold yourself. A good rule is when you are in doubt, ask questions.

Back to trust

This chapter first focused on trust, then moved on to congruence, and finally settled for a moment on the question of context. Before I close I want to come back to trust. It is so important! Let me offer further encouragement that you develop a sense of trust. A developing sense of trust will give you:

▶ the will, and the ability, to keep on growing;

▶ help in establishing solid personal values while you learn how to examine and reexamine those values from time to time to see if they are still useful;

▶ the ability to recognize the wonderfully complex being you are and will help you evaluate the many different and exhilarating thoughts, feelings, and actions of which you are capable;

▶ more and more self-respect that leads to acceptance of yourself—and then others;

▶ freedom to make decisions, claim ownership of them, and find joy in what you have decided;

▶ a push forward to meet life head-on—with confidence.

Erik Erikson is right; claiming a sense of personal trust is one of the primary tasks of life. The more you dig around in that world of building of trust, while claiming for yourself the benefits it contains, the more trustworthy you become.

The Lord Jesus Christ said, "I have come that they may have life, and have it to the full" (John 10:10). The full life Jesus talks about is directly linked to trust. It begins with trusting him. As we trust him, believing that he intended we should have a fulfilling life, believing that he meant the full life for each one of us, believing that he has made a fulfilling life possible through his earned forgiveness, believing that he will be with us, and in us, each day of our life, we will get closer to a biblical understanding of trust (whether of self or others) and its importance in our life. That's true. Trust me. I do.

Five

OUT OF YOUR SHELL

When a Broadway playwright finishes a script he or she sells it to a New York producer. Then a whole series of things starts happening. A director is chosen. Actors are selected for all the parts. Sets are designed. The entire cast begins rehearsing. Can you guess what happens next? They take the play on the road to cities outside of New York—Boston, Philadelphia, Baltimore, or Washington, D.C.—and try out their production.

During the trial run the playwright, the director, and the actors make adjustments in the production based on the response of the audience, the comments of the critics and their own "feel" for how things are going. They try to see their effort through eyes of others and also sift it through their own experienced sensitivities. All the while they make adjustments.

Sometimes the play that opened in Boston is never presented on Broadway. The participants decide that their effort is not good enough and the show closes far from Broadway. But other times they discover in places like D.C. that they have a hit on their hands. If that's the case, they pack up and head for the bright lights of "New York, New York, that wonderful town," as the song says.

These trial runs of theatrical extravaganzas are similar to the practice, studying, testing, experimentation, and changing that everyone makes (and ought to make!) during the teenage years. The teen years are a kind of "out-of-town-opening" for the life you will stage before the world in the years to come.

I don't want to suggest that living in the teenage years is some kind of holding pattern, a less-than-real experience. No way! You are alive and living—really living—right now! The things you do, the things that happen to you, and the things you do to others emphatically influence what you and others will be in the future. Yet, these teenage years are unique in that you get a chance to present your ideas, experiment with patterns of action, test various responses, make appropriate changes, and do all that in circumstances that are not quite as critically consequential as some periods later in your life. You can make adjustments without severe dislocations in the lives of others, as will later be the case. You can learn lessons of great value that will be useful in all the years ahead. How you learn these lessons, when you learn these lessons, and the price you pay to learn these lessons, are all part of the continuing growth of the teenage years.

A larger audience and a more complicated plot

When you were a little kid, did you and several friends ever decide to put on a play in your basement and invite neighborhood folks, family, and friends to attend? Many of us did that. It was fun. We got lots of applause, lots of compliments, and lots of ice cream for our effort.

It's one thing to put on a very amateurish play in your basement, for those who know and like you, but quite another thing to test your theatrical skills on a full-sized stage before a large, unknown, and potentially unfriendly audience. In a very real sense you make the very first moves out of the little basement of family onto the unknown and potentially dangerous public stage during the teens. You will do that right now.

Remember what that first "performance" before the friendly, basement audience was like? They reacted positively to everything you did. They told you—and kept telling you—how great you were, how cute you were, how much ability you had. Oh, someone may have made a hurtful comment or said something that was hard to take. But you always knew they were on your side and weren't out to cause you any real harm. No real problem there.

Then came the day you figuratively moved out of your basement "theater" onto the larger stage of your neighborhood. That happened about the time you started going to school. Your audience expanded. It now included your "gang," the tight-knit little group of two or three (sometimes a few more) with whom you could test out some of your ideas and feelings. They too, were basically a very friendly audience. Wasn't that some more fun? Hanging around and acting wild with all of them was a pastime full of delight.

Guess what? You moved on. Look out world! Here you come. You moved onto the stage of the teen years and junior high or middle school. The big time! More people in the audience! Many more people! Instead of having just one teacher (a critic, maybe?) who taught you all day long, and who knew everything there was to know about you, you now had a half dozen or more who individually judged you and responded to your skills in different ways. Instead of very close contact with only a few friends your circle of acquaintance expanded to 10, 20, 30, 40 or maybe 50 individuals. Is that now? Is the audience to whom you play getting larger every day? How about the production? Much more complicated? I'm sure that's true. The demands of your "part" are getting more challenging. With it all the possibilities of failure, or glorious success, dangle before your eyes.

To further complicate the whole matter, don't you sense

an inner desire (even though a carefully-hidden inner desire) to show others the great stuff you feel you really have? Do you notice any secret yearnings to reach out for even bigger and better things? Maybe yes?

Now don't let me confuse you. The relative size of the stage and the audience you deal with may be very different when compared to other's aspirations. Maybe all you want to be is home room student council representative (your stage), while another yearns to be chosen as a page in the U.S. Senate (theirs)! The point of comparison is the constant seeking for something more than what you have had and a place larger than where you have acted before. You yearn for more and larger. That whole churning yearning has a name: *social group readiness*. Social group readiness reaches its peak sometime in the teenage years. Like most other things that surface during those exciting eight years, social group readiness comes to some earlier and to others later. Only if the feeling doesn't come at all is something wrong. Even then it can be helped. Lest I confuse you by saying too little about social group readiness let me share a bit more.

Social group readiness includes wanting to meet new people. It involves seeking and being willing to accept different leadership roles in school, church, and in the community. Whenever it comes, social group readiness signals for the vast majority of teenagers a breaking out of tight and exclusive family bonds and of limited neighborhood groupings. Teens who have achieved social group readiness reach out for more associations with all kinds of people, some their own age and some older. This period often scares parents. They tend to think their son or daughter is not mature enough to act on a larger stage. Maybe you are. Maybe you aren't. But the feeling is there to be recognized and dealt with whether your folks accept it or not. You are the one who senses it.

One of my friends describes this reaching out to others as "the expanding web of friendship." He developed that term while watching a spider at work. As the spider spun the web, making it larger and larger, the little creature was actually expanding its world. Each strand of the web became the platform from which the spider reached out to weave the next strand. Every new strand gave the spider an opportunity to weave a larger and larger web. From each effort the spider gained experience about how to reach further. In a sense, through its efforts, the spider was expanding its world.

You do much the same thing. You move from one grouping of friends to another, and then to another, and yet another. This expanding web of friendship and contact with other people is working all the time. You meet a friend who introduces you to someone else who then invites you to a party. There you meet others who invite you to join a club where you make more friends. Your world of social action is on the move. When you are socially ready your world expands at a marvelous speed. It keeps involving more people and the relationships take on new and exciting complexity. Socially-ready people like it that way.

One test of your social readiness can be made at your next youth gathering. Determine ahead of time that at the next youth gathering you attend you will actively seek to do two things: (1) limit the time you spend with your "group," and (2) seek new acquaintances. On the stage from which I speak I can easily spot who is ready and who is not. The ready ones are having a great time. The unready ones sit in the back row, or off to the side, with their little bunch. It's more fun when you are ready. You lose none of the old. You gain much that is new.

What about me?

The expansion of the web of friendship is exciting, but you can get lost in the process. You can be so busy meeting, talking, sharing, and "performing" on this larger stage that you forget about yourself. Somehow you lose your identity—your sense of self. You are so busy playing a part that you forget to be a person. How can you take care of that problem?

While the web of friendship is expanding and your on-stage time is extending, it is important to recognize that you need to spend some time by yourself. Too much time alone would turn you into a loner. It would take you off the stage entirely and out of the web of friendship. At the same time, too little time alone turns you into a kind of social butterfly flitting everywhere and settling nowhere. While busily touching the lives of others, you become unaware of your own needs.

Time alone? Why time alone? You need time alone to unscramble those many new experiences you are undergoing. You need time, through reflection, for "reading the reviews" (that's what actors do when they check out what the critics have to say about their performance). By reading your reviews and making judgments about them, you develop a sensitivity that is best expressed by the writer of Ecclesiastes: "For everything there is a season, a time for every matter under heaven" (Eccles. 3:1). You realize that there is a time to be with others and a time to be by yourself; a time to tell others what you think and a time to listen to what they have to say; a time to be guided by the comments of friends and a time to make your own judgment; a time to reflect on what ought to be changed and a time to stand fast on what should remain.

One good check on how to evaluate things in your time of private reflection is to remember a simple truth: at the very top of your list of best friends should be you! Jesus said, "Love your neighbor as yourself" (Mark 12:31). You can't love others unless you also love yourself. If you don't love the person who is your closest neighbor—you—how will you ever be able to love the many other "neighbors" you meet each day? While loving others is the finest expression of the human life, that love of others grows out of a loving understanding and acceptance of yourself.

I am responsible for you—and me

In those quiet times of evaluation, you will come to recognize that the groups with whom you associate affect how you think, how you feel, and how you act. Some call this peer pressure. The influence of peers can be positive or negative. Which is it for you? How do others affect you? Are you easily manipulated, like a piece of soft clay? Can you be led to do anything the group wants you to do? Are you a manipulator always wanting things your way? Whatever you answer, you have a significant effect on your group, for good or evil. Recognizing the seriousness of the effects of your actions ought to make you constantly rethink your plan. Should you bravely push on, or moderate what you are doing?

I saw this dynamic in action a few summers ago at the Dakota Boys Ranch near Minot, North Dakota. The boys (all of whom come from troubled home circumstances) live in separate cottages—about a dozen to each building. Counselors live with them not only to control them but to help them grow in self-control. The rules of the facility are based on teamwork. What one boy in a cottage does touches everyone in the cottage. When one needs help, all pitch in. When one is intimidated, all must face the consequences. It's quite a place to visit. Their rules of interaction build young men who can relate in and to the world.

There were two boys at a residential treatment center for the emotionally disturbed. The boys and I were talking together about the question, "What can one person do to make this a better place to live?" The boys thought it was a strange question. They had never considered anything like that before. They had only thought about what others should be doing to improve their condition. After hearing the question, the boys made a fascinating decision.

These two boys decided that although what they did seemed to have little effect on the other 22 in their dormitory they would form a small group dedicated to improve their living conditions. They decided that this small group should work at developing a sense of positive, helpful action, to improve their life. What started with two expanded to four, and before long spread through the entire unit. Stemming from the action of those two all the others joined in cleaning their dormitory. They gained permission to paint their rooms. And would you believe it, they quit blaming others for their living conditions? They did such a good job and got so much support that today their living quarters are fully carpeted and much improved. It all happened because two boys decided they were responsible for themselves *and* responsible to the people who lived with them.

I could tell you stories of the opposite—two or three in a class who decided to tear things up and got others to help them. Have you ever been in a room where a couple of kids decided to disrupt the learning situation by horsing around, disobeying, or constantly breaking the educational spell so that nothing could happen? Ever heard of a small group that decided to be totally uncooperative at school meetings so that any student government effort is doomed to failure, or who organized to "crash" a party or disrupt a dance? Amazing as it may seem, it takes organization, will, and commitment to do those destructive things, just as it takes organization, will, and commitment to do positive things. All the "destroyers" show is that they are not socially ready to become part of a responsible group. They aren't sensitive to needs of others. In your private time think about all this. Life circumstances are never neutral. There are no vacuums. Either you are affecting or are being affected. Which?

Picking a pattern

All of us learn much from the example of others. We learn most, and fastest, from our friends. Gradually, over the years, each of us choose a pattern of conduct and establish our own personal style—but it will be based on what we have picked up from friends. In your web of friendship, you try out many different things, test your feelings, experiment, and endeavor to influence your surrounding as much as it influences you.

At first you test out with friends what you learned from home ("my dad says . . . "). But if dad's insight seems to apply to a former era his influence gives way to the wisdom of friends. By the words and examples of your circle of friends you learn about life: clothing, music, sports, and how to treat members of the opposite sex. You determine what to wear, and how you want to wear it. You decide whether you should learn to play the guitar, the piano, or the bass. You are guided in the records you buy. You learn the latest dance from others. Watching others, you also make decisions about your hair style, your expressions and language patterns, the movies to attend, the right places to go.

As the years pass, the questions you answer become more complex. Shall I buy a car? What's the best career in life? Do I want to go to college? Who should I date? Most of your answers are developed from the experiences, the understandings, and the shaping you received from your friends. Friends. Friends are important. They are your surest potential source of enormous support and finest example.

By treating you, your ideas, and your ideal with respect, friends also have a way of confirming you as a real person. Do you remember how you felt when a friend first asked you for advice? When your friend followed your advice and thanked you for it later, you felt even better. That's how friends recognize the value of your judgment. They also show you are trustworthy. What better proof of trustworthiness than a friend telling you an important secret! Friends also reinforce you as a person when they say, "Help me!" It could mean, "Help me mend by broken heart." It could mean, "Help me to shore." It could mean, "Help me understand algebra." Whatever the way you are asked to help, it means someone has confidence in you. What a good feeling! That action of a friend helps you sense how lovable and capable you are as a human being. Friends develop love, confidence, trust, and respect within you. Friends make you grow as a person in the same way that water, sunshine, and rich soil cause the flowers to bloom.

But like most things in life, there is another side to the story! Friends, good friends, may also present a problem.

I like it! I want more!

Friends may not only make you feel good, they may make you feel too good. They can be like sugar. While sugar adds taste to the world of eating, too much causes tooth decay, or gives you a figure that only a mother would love. You need to keep your sugar intake balanced or you will be in for some serious, negative side effects.

In this same way a limited amount of group reinforcement can be supportive and help you grow. The danger is that you may get to like group support so much that you push on for more, and more, and more. One term for that yearning is called "a quest for popularity." Yearning for popularity may make you do things you thought you would never do. The pressure of wanting popularity may make you so hungry for recognition that you feel cheated when you don't get it—or when someone else gets the recognition you want. You may start testing the group to become what they seek and be guided by what they want. When that happens you may think you're doing a good job of taking care of yourself, but you aren't. You are really failing yourself, and you aren't being very helpful to the group, either.

Growth in a group comes from healthy and honest inter-action. Things should be happening between you and other people in such a way that no one wins all the time (or loses) and both parties are improved. The most important contri-bution you may make to the group is not what they want, but what they need. And the most important thing for yourself may not be what you want to do, but what you ought to do.

Healthy interaction focuses more on "need" than "want." In that kind of exchange, popularity is not a goal. It is a result.

Anyone who pushes for popularity and forgets responsibility usually loses the very thing they are after. Few people are as unpopular as those who want to be popular no matter what. The popularity-hungry person may have a moment of glory, but that moment won't last long. After group members see how little self-respect that popularity-hungry person has, and how little trust he has in the group's judgment, the sought for popularity actually wanes and often disappears. It doesn't take long to understand that one who must always be stage center, doesn't really love himself. The spotlights that show his personal plusses also highlight his flaws. Why make a fool of himself while showing off? He shouldn't be so mean to his "me." And if someone doesn't love himself, how can he really love someone else?

Real popularity comes by itself, as each person deserves it. Do the things that earn recognition from your group, and popularity will be laid at your feet, sought or not. It may not be the kind of popularity you envision, but it will certainly be the kind you really need—and the kind that you can handle.

I'm going to share more about this whole area in Chapter 7 under the subject of coping. Give some extra thought to these last few paragraphs so that you'll really be ready for what's to come.

Stop showing

The "super-popular-living-on-the-center-of-the-stage" roles are pressure positions. It's like being at the front of the kids who are trying to get through the halls between classes. The nearer the front you are, the greater the pressure of the group behind you. Being popular exposes you to one of the most powerful forces in the world—"group pressure." Some also call it "peer pressure." What power in pressure! Pay attention! Look out!

As a demonstration of the power of group pressure a psychologist showed some people a series of lines on a paper, one of which was shorter than the other. Before the entire group was gathered, most of them were privately instructed to insist that every line was identical in length. Would you believe that those who weren't told this eventually actually agreed that every line was identical in length, even though they later admitted they knew it wasn't so! They said they agreed because everyone else thought so. Group pressure made them deny what they saw with their eyes.

Group pressure does strange things to people. Some teenagers wear clothes they don't like, listen to records they don't appreciate, attend movies they don't appreciate, participate in sexual activities they don't agree with, use drugs they don't enjoy—all because "everyone else" says it's the thing to do. Group pressure can be frightening. What can you do about it?

What I want to share with you in the next few paragraphs is repeated in other ways through the book. It needs to be repeated. It is so true that forgetting it for even a few moments can have disastrous consequences for your life. Here it is: The best protection against damaging group pressure are clearly drawn personal boundaries of right and wrong. Actually these personal boundaries are God's Ten Commandments . . . applied. Set the boundaries. Make them strong and sturdy. Later in life you may adjust one or the other to your changed circumstance, but right now it's important to have these boundaries as a protection to your sense of self-worth. If you have a weak set of moral boundaries surrounding your sense of worth, group pressure may become irresistibly powerful. Build those boundaries. Put a high value on yourself.

One thing that helps me in my sense of worth, and in understanding the usefulness of boundaries, is to remember how valuable I am to God and how God sees me. God loves me so much that he gave up what must be the second most precious thing he has: his Son. The thought of eternity without you and me in heaven moved God to establish a plan of salvation unequalled in human memory. God did this for us. Now, in love, he encourages me to act responsibly in Spirit-led response to what he first did for us. Knowing that God loves me, and loves me as I am, helps me to put a proper price tag on myself. The more I appreciate God's value of me, the stronger I become as a person. The stronger I become as a person, the stronger is my resistance to group pressures. When I know God and I are right, the group has to be wrong.

Summary? Resist destructive group pressures by beginning at the level of your God-given self-esteem. When you have a good understanding of who you are you will be able to handle the forces that try to chip away at your values.

I wish I had some friends

I've been talking about friends and friendship groups as if everyone has them. That may not be true. You may be terribly lonely because you don't have any real friends. What do you do if you want a friend and don't have one? What do you do if you want to belong to a group and can't get in?

The best way to get a friend is to be a friend. It may be easier said than done, especially if you want to be a friend of someone who apparently doesn't want to be a friend to you. But it is not impossible to develop a friendship even in that strange circumstance. Take it a step at a time.

First, choose someone you would like to have as a friend. Choose carefully. Then be that person's friend. I don't mean that you should "buy" friendship by giving unusual gifts or fawning over them. I mean be a friend. Help when you can. Talk with the person. It may be helpful to make this effort with two or three persons at the same time. That way if the moment is not right with one person, it could be right with another. The most important thing is to keep on being a friend. There are more than enough people around who want a friend. Look for one or more. If you try, you can become the friend they want, and they will be the friends you desire.

If things really get tough, get some help. There are people who really want to be your friend: a teacher, a minister, a youth leader, another person at school. They are ready to share their experiences. When I need friendly help, I often turn to people who are much older than am I. They don't think of me as a nuisance, or inferior, or some weakling. They accept me at face value as one who wants to be their friend, and as one who wants them as a friend. I have found that the older the person I reach out to, the more likely I will have a pleasant and positive experience. Young people usually get along well with their grandparents because they have so much in common. When people get on toward the later years of their life they see things much more clearly and treasure the really important things much more highly than when they were younger. Older guys like me make great friends.

Fall back on your faith

This time of learning to be a friend is also an excellent time to review your Christian faith. The two work hand in hand. Work through things you have been taught in the past and which you now say that you believe. Study the Scriptures. Walking through the Word of God helps put many things in proper focus. The Bible gives you a positive and encouraging picture of yourself. You see yourself as the pardoned, forgiven, and loved human being that you are. The Bible helps you see others in the same light as well.

Scripture does not picture life as a series of treacherous events all intent on destroying you. Quite the contrary. Life is presented as God's great gift to you. Jesus said, "I have come that they may have life, and have it to the full" (John 10:10). God wants you to have life, a fulfilling life. He's not just talking about heaven! The Creator who once said about all his divine action, "It is good," knows how great life can and should be. Let God lead you to the better! Walk with God under the judgment and mercy he puts upon you, with a sure understanding of your weaknesses and his strength. You will learn to be a friend, and have a friend, and to live successfully in the context of all your friendships. You will discover how to be a blessing to others and how others can be a blessing to you.

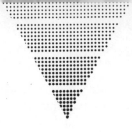

Six

HEAR WHAT OTHERS SPEAK— SPEAK SO OTHERS CAN HEAR

Have you ever had a problem with communication? A young man I know asked his father a simple question: "Dad, are you using the car this afternoon?" Wham! Bam!—an atomic explosion! His father erupted in anger, yelled at him for always wanting the car, cut him down as unreasonable and irresponsible, and told him (and what seemed like the whole world) that there were other people in the family who might enjoy using that automobile sometime. It got embarrassing when the dust settled and dad finally understood the question. All my friend wanted to know was whether the car would be available that afternoon so he could wash it in appreciation for the many times he used it. Bad communication.

I heard about a shy guy who was once innocently asked by a girl, "Do you have a date for the senior prom?" He thought she was inviting him to be her date. That wasn't her intention. She was just curious—and concerned about him. Before it was finally straightened out both had to struggle through an awkward experience involving an innocently garbled message. The cause? Bad communication!

It seems to me that about half the movies you see, especially the ones we call "situation comedies," spin out a story line based on a verbal misunderstanding, or some other mistake in the communication process. You know how it works: first, someone misunderstands a message, then everyone else in the movie hilariously compounds the miscommunication for an hour or more. There's nothing new about that story line. Shakespeare used it. So has almost every other great writer in history. Whether in classical literature or on TV soaps, bad communication generates human problems. By contrast the opposite is true, too: good communication helps.

Communication is crucial

Life, all of it, pivots around communicating and communication skills. From learning to say our first words, on to struggling over writing a couple of coherent, connectable sentences, to the present when we seem to spend half our time explaining what we really meant to say, communication has been a needed skill at the center of our existence. Since it's so central (and it is) we need to focus on it for a bit.

Where do we start? Let's start at ground zero: communication means much more than making words whether the words are written or spoken. Communication is a process for sharing ideas, desires, information, thoughts, and feelings by means of written and spoken words, art, facial expressions, body language, or any other means.

Communication is at its best when we express ourselves so clearly that the other person fully comprehends the message we are sending. Communication at its worst not only doesn't get the correct and intended message through, it projects an unintended and confusing one. Communication—good communication—is hard! But it doesn't always have to be. At least it doesn't have to be as bad as it sometimes is! Not if we work at it. So let's do it. Let's concentrate on communication. We begin at the beginning.

What does communication mean?

The word *communicate* means, literally, "to hold in common." When you have shared an idea with someone else in such a way that he fully understands and "holds in common" that idea with you, communication has happened. In its simplest form communication is a way of reaching out to others.

Communication is also the doorway through which you let other people peek into you. Communication failures imprison us within ourselves. Imprisoned behind the walls of poor communication we are unable to share feelings, express love, offer help, stir response. At this very moment we (that's me and you) are going through a communication struggle. I'm working hard to communicate with you! I want you to see inside of me and come to know my deepest feelings. I want to get my ideas inside of you. I want you to get my message. I'm depending on you working just as hard at understanding my efforts. If we both do a good job communication, will happen. If either fails, neither succeeds.

Words and deeds and other things

Many things contribute to the communication process—and complicate it! The tone of your voice, the inflection of your speech, your posture, your word selection, your facial expression, and the loudness of your voice, just to mention a few things, all affect it. Would you believe that even punctuation can be a problem? Let me show you what I mean. Look at these words:

Woman without her man is nothing.

What does that sentence mean? Do you know? In an experiment men and women participants were asked to punctuate that sentence so that it made sense to them. Most women punctuated the sentence this way:

Woman, without her, man is nothing.

And the men? They punctuated it:

Woman without her man, is nothing.

The words of each sentence are identical. But the placement of the comma(s) makes a big difference.

Commas can be erased, shifted around, or even omitted. But how do you adjust for a frown? A growl? An explosively loud voice? A pat on the back? Someone walking away? A sneer? How do you punctuate emotional words like "cry baby," "sissy," "delinquent," "squeal," and hundreds of others so that the wrong message is not sent? The words you use and the way you use them influence the receiver's understanding of your message. Look at these two sentences.

1. She squealed on him.
2. She acted responsibly and reported him to the proper authorities.

Both sentences describe the same action, but the words used make for a very different message!

The point of this section? All people (you included) communicate not only verbally but nonverbally. Words, looks, punctuation, tone of voice all "speak." The way you construct a sentence, whether you smile as you speak, whether you are looking another in the eye or turning your back—all of those things communicate. They communicate at least something. Are you convinced that this is a complicated process? It gets even more complicated when you send two messages at the same time.

When words and deeds don't match

Two messages? At the same time? Unless you are careful, you do that. You can send a verbal message and a nonverbal message simultaneously. That's common in conversation. The words (verbal) are reinforced by the tone of your voice (nonverbal). Imagine someone saying, "Stop that!" to you. Depending on the circumstance, you would need to hear the voice and see the face of the speaker to know what that simple message means.

Take it a step further. What if a speaker sends two *conflicting* messages at the same time—the verbal message saying one thing and the nonverbal something else. That's when misunderstandings multiply and relationships deteriorate. Example? Let me share two.

1. Your boyfriend says, "I think you're the greatest girl in the world." Clear message? What if he doesn't take you home to meet his mother? Two messages. Which is for real? All you can do is guess.

2. What if someone applies for a job dressed sloppily, with eyes down and chin on chest, and answers all questions with "uh huh" or "unh uh," or sounds like he doesn't care? What's the message? Does the applicant want the job? He did come. Is the problem that he has very little self-confidence? Is that why his eyes are averted and he has his chin on his chest? Maybe he doesn't want the job and came only because his parents made him—hence the sloppy clothes? Of the two being sent, what's the real message? I don't know.

I believe all people (me, too!) intentionally send confusing and conflicting messages. Sometimes. We do this because we think we will then be "safe" regardless of how the receiver responds to us. If the receiver interprets our message in a way that turns out good we can say, "Yeah! Yeah! That's what I meant." If the receiver argues with our suggestion, makes fun of our idea, or puts it down in any way, we can always say, "I didn't mean that at all." My favorite example of conflicting communication is a girl asking her father for a dress (or anything else that's important to her). He sends two messages with one word: "Maybe." What does that mean? Maybe yes? Maybe no? Should she plan to get the dress? Should she buy material to make one of her own? What's she supposed to do? His "maybe" is confusing, conflicting, and unfair. In addition it doesn't help.

We'll deal with this a little later again but it fits right here, too: the best way to handle people who send conflicting messages is to press for further explanation. Make him say yes or no. If the young woman in the example presses she may learn that her father meant, "If I had the money, I'd be glad to buy you a dress. But I don't have the money." With that as an answer she can plan. But those blankety-blank *maybes* are the stuff from which broken hearts, broken dreams, and broken relationships are made. No need for any of it!

I was once the victim (largely my own fault I must admit) of conflicting communication with our oldest daughter. When she was in junior high her mother and I told her to wear anklets to school. She didn't want to. She never really explained her reluctance. About all we got out of her was that anklets "were dumb." But she obeyed. Somewhat. To a point. Every morning she put on her anklets and went off to school. But every afternoon, coming back from school, she'd be barefooted, carrying her shoes and her socks. Her explanation for this unusual behavior was, "It's fun to go barefooted." Now I may be stupid sometimes, but I'm not dumb. I suspected that something was wrong. Yet, I couldn't get a clearly communicated response from her to my question about why she didn't want to wear anklets. After thinking it over I confronted her. I told her that I was going to park by the school at the end of the day and check the students as they left. If half the girls wore anklets, she would have to wear them too. But if less than half did. . . .

Came the afternoon I parked in front of the school and watched the students leave. I immediately understood. *None of the girls wore anklets!* Not one. That's what my daughter had been trying to communicate to me. Because I could only remember how pretty her mother had looked to me when she was wearing anklets in high school her terse message about

THANK GOD I'M A TEENAGER

anklets being "dumb" confused me. We could have been spared some family grief if she had spoken more clearly or if I had taken the time to develop a clear response. The lesson to me in that experience is good communication needs good senders and good receivers.

Senders and receivers

It's so important let me say it again: good communication needs a clear message-sender and a sensitive message-receiver. Without both, communication is difficult.

As the sender, it is your responsibility to forward messages that can be easily understood. Be sure the verbal and nonverbal message matches. I can't say to my children, "I have something very important to tell you" as I pass through the room and go outside. They will never understand how serious the message is. My nonverbal action does not match the verbal message.

The same rule applies to receivers. You can't slump in a chair before a blaring TV and say, "I'm listening." You may be listening very carefully, but in that moment the sender doesn't know that. If you are actually listening very carefully, you must send a nonverbal reinforcement that proves it: look the speaker in the eye—and turn down the TV.

Checking out the message

Good receivers (that means they are friendly, hardworking, and conscientious) will always check out the message they have heard. Suppose the following conversation took place between you and a friend:

FRIEND: See you tonight!
YOU: Sure!

Any possibility of confusion there? I mean, if that conversational segment were allowed to stand, without anyone checking out what it means, is there any possibility of confusion? You better believe it! A lot!

Let's replay that conversation in the long-play version. It could come out like this:

FRIEND: See you tonight!

YOU: Sure! I can hardly wait to hear the new band.

FRIEND: Band? What band? Is there going to be a band at church?

YOU: Church? I'm not talking about church. I'm talking about the ninth grade dance. Isn't that where you were going to meet me?

FRIEND: No. I mean the church. Remember? Tonight at the church? Don't you remember? The youth group program committee meets and we're both on it.

YOU: Oops! I forgot all about that! Now what will I do?

I don't know what *You* is going to do, but I know that the real message finally got through. And when real messages get through, you're in better shape to make the most appropriate response, whatever that may be.

I once asked my son to clean the car. He agreed. That's all we said. When I got home the car wasn't clean. What had happened? Was he lazy? Disobedient? Thoughtless? None of those three. Our problem was communication. My son thought I wanted the car cleaned by the weekend because he knew his mom and I were going out. Wrong! I wanted the car cleaned by the time I got home because his mother and I had to pick up some people and take them to a party. That night! Who was at fault? Both, actually. I hadn't sent a clear message. I could have been more complete. He didn't act out the part of a good receiver because he didn't check out the message I sent. We both assumed we held something in common—and we didn't.

Try checking out all messages you receive for the next few days. Every time you get a message, feed back what you heard. You will be amazed how often you misunderstood; how often you didn't get the whole message. If you make that effort, and start training yourself to check out messages, you will spare yourself great chunks of grief for the rest of your life. And you will have learned one of the fundamental rules of good communication.

Silence isn't always golden

Some people say silence is golden. I don't agree. Silence can be very confusing. I've mentioned that painful question I get from many teens: "Why can't my parents say, 'I love you'?" Not much "gold" in the parental silence there! Not unless you call the cry of inner pain "golden." Yet, sad to say, silence is one of our more common communicators. Sound odd to you? Think of it; by keeping silent we are often very eloquent. Silence is loud. The difficulty is that no one really knows what all the loud silence means. Is someone "silently" saying, "I am sick"? Or is the silence a signal of disinterest? Or agreement? Or boredom? Anger, maybe? Fright? Or, what? Who knows? Only you, the silent one, know for sure.

One reason your parents get so curious about what you are doing, and seem to question every one of your experiences, is that you're not yet a very good communicator. At least, most teenagers aren't. Do you give a little grunt here, a shake of the shoulder there, or stand silently saying nothing? When you go out for two hours, come back in, walk up to your room and close the door what's the message? It's a conversation with no words. What are you trying to say with all those "no words"? Pretty tough figuring out a "no words" conversation.

Don't forget; when we are silent we're placing all the communication responsibility on the other person. "Let 'em guess!" Our silence locks people out of our thoughts, excludes them from the world of our feelings, leaves them guessing about what we really mean, and chokes off communication. Pretty deadly.

Don't use silence as a means for communicating unless you actually intend to confuse. If that's what you mean to do, be assured silence will do a good job. But its unfair and actually counter-productive. It ricochets and, as my North Carolina friends say, "You gits what you gives." Your confusing silence invites a confusing response. Be nicer to yourself.

Unplug those ears

The flip side of not speaking is not listening. Not listening can be just as destructive and dangerous as not speaking. When you don't listen, you keep missing the messages others are sending to you. Some of those messages are important. Unplugged ears brighten communication. You start hearing things you've missed before.

Over the years, one of my children has called me by various names. "Dad" was the most common name and meant nothing more than that she wanted my attention. "Daddy" usually meant she was going to tease me or share something not too serious. When she called me "father" she was telling me the matter had some significance to her. But "papa" was her signal things were very serious. By being sensitive to those various words, by "unplugging my ears," I learned how to prepare myself for her messages and to give them the appropriate attention. I'm not such a great parent, but I do listen.

One of the worst communication sins any of us commit (all of us some time . . . some of us all the time) is that of actually tuning people out. We don't hear them. As soon as they begin to speak we block their every word. It's not easy to not-hear. It takes years of training to master the art. Don't let yourself slip into the habit of tuning people out. We usually fall into a not-hearing pattern with those who are closest to us, the very ones who least deserve it from us, and who have the most to share with us. Make listening a habit. Consciously perk up your ears.

Send it direct

If you want to pass a message to someone else, the best way to do it is by sending it direct. Don't send it via a third party or try to bounce it off a fourth person. Say it directly to the person to whom you want to send the message. That way you know if it got through or went astray. Miles Standish, the military leader of the Pilgrims, learned that indirect messages are a poor means of communication. He learned the hard way. He asked John Alden to propose to Priscilla Mullins on his behalf. Priscilla ended up married to John. What would have happened if Miles had gone himself? No one knows for sure, but things couldn't have turned out more badly for Miles than when he did it the wrong way his first—and only—time.

Your parents, your pastor, your teachers, and other adults are confused by indirect teenage messages. When they hear indirectly what one or the other teenager would like to have they wonder, "Why didn't he talk with me?" They sometimes take an indirect communication process as a personal affront. By the same token, teenagers tell me they often send indirect messages because they are afraid of the answer they might receive, or they feel awkward in their request, or they aren't sure how to express themselves. Lay those concerns aside. Jump in. Go directly to the person. If your words are clumsy, then trust that your actions (another means of communication) will help clear up any confusion in communication. Trust me. No matter what happens, direct is best.

Keep the facts straight

Facts are friends. They help the communication process. When you have the facts, communicate the facts, and keep the facts straight, you help another person hear. I didn't understand my daughter's phrase, "It's dumb!" when I asked why she didn't want to wear anklets. There were no facts in her statement. And, at first, there were no facts in my response. Without the facts, it's no wonder her message got confused.

To help communication in your home you may want to look at Chapter 2 again and review distortions about teenagers. Are your parents operating with any of those myths, assuming that they are factual? That could confuse communication. Help them get the facts straight.

When you ask something of your parents, be sure you have the facts and present them clearly. You could be in trouble by only asking, "May I go out next Tuesday?" There are some facts in that request, but not many. Instead, why don't you tell the whole story? Say, "I'd like to go out next Tuesday night. We're not going to have school on Wednesday, so it won't conflict with my schoolwork. I'll be going with Greg and Jim. We want to check out the price of jeans at the new store on the mall. We'll be back at nine. Greg's dad is taking us and picking us up again after he's through bowling." All those facts will help your parents clearly hear your request and hopefully respond more favorably.

Communicating something negative

Not all vital communication is fun-and-games stuff. Sometimes you need to communicate tough stuff: a correction, a reprimand, a rejection, a refusal. That's part of life. How about the need to communicate appropriate anger, frustration, or disappointment? How do you send a negative message?

First of all, the communication of negatives really has to be person to person. Commend in public, or through another, but correct in private, face-to-face. A third party describing the intensity of your negative emotions will only confuse the matter. Isn't that what happens when mom tries to tell you how mad dad is about something you have done? When you next meet dad you don't know how to react. It usually turns out badly.

Second, any negative message must be completely factual. Say what made you angry, or what you'd like to see changed, or why you are disappointed.

Third, strip that negative message of insulting words before you send it. When someone starts out a conversation by calling me a name, I have a hard time hearing the rest of the message no matter how important or accurate it may be. If you want to communicate with me, don't begin by embarrassing me.

Fourth, carefully select the words you use when sending a negative message. Let the words you chose focus on the action you find unacceptable without attacking the person involved. The rejection of the action itself is bad enough, but when you shift from negative action to the negativeness of the person, ears instantly close and the whole communication process grinds to a halt.

Fifth (and this is so essential), after you send a negative message let the other person know you care about them. Remember, there is a "person" inside that one to whom you sent the message. Let that person know your feelings. Recently I heard my youngest daughter confront her older sister about borrowing personal items without asking. It was a straight-forward, person-to-person, nonblaming, triple-E message (you'll learn more about them a bit later). At the end of her confrontation she gave her sister a soft, caring look and said, "I'm not mad at you. I love you, but I want you to know how I feel about your borrowing my clothes without asking." The negative message was clear. The caring message was clearer yet. It worked. Try it!

As Christ did

Jesus was a master of communication. He sent highly complex, and often critical, messages but used very simple, caring words. As you read the Bible note how often he checked out the messages he heard and also those he sent. One way he did this was by asking questions after he had spoken. Another way was by telling a parable, or a story, to underline his point of communication. He many times requested a readback with questions like, "Who do men say that I am?" (Mark 8:27).

When he did attack people (and sometimes he did), it was because the person and the person's action were so totally interwoven that there was no way of separating them. But he more commonly rejected an action without rejecting the person(s) involved.

The key to all Christ's communication is an openly expressed intent on his part of earning and offering salvation for everyone. He offered it to all through forgiveness. He sent that message a hundred times or more. Whether he was confronting Judas person-to-person, or checking out the intention of the questioning lawyer, or trying to get the facts straight with a woman caught in adultery, he did it desiring to communicate. He worked hard at communicating. If only he had been surrounded by better listeners! If only he had better listeners today! Regardless of the past he still wants to communicate with you. Listen to him. Did you hear what I said?

Seven

COPING—AND MUCH MORE

This is one of the most important chapters in this book. It responds to a common teenage inner question, "Will I ever get all the pieces of my life in their proper place? Can all the ideas of this book work—for me?" The answer is an emphatic yes! The way you make it all work is by *applying the secret principles of life*. Actually, these principles are secret only to those who have not yet discovered them. So they are not so secret after all, though not everyone who reads this book will discover them. Their detection requires a maturity and a basic wholeness which some haven't attained yet. But since you were mature and whole enough to read this far you're very likely ready to discover and claim the secret principles of life. Let's see.

Have beliefs

We started this book with Christopher Columbus. Remember? And remember how we said that at the time of his great discovery he probably didn't know where he was or how he got there? Well, true as all that may be, there's more to be said for him than that! He had a belief. While others believed the world was flat, he believed it was round. While others said the way to India was by sailing east, he believed you could get there by sailing west. I'm certain he wasn't the first man who thought that, but he was one of the first to do something about it. You see, Christopher Columbus (1) had beliefs, (2) held to his beliefs under pressure, and (3) acted on them! One. Two. Three. Those are some of the "secrets" this chapter is about. But there are more.

Recognize truth and lies

Underpinning Christopher's actions was an ability to recognize the difference between reality and illusion. Was the world flat, like everybody else said, or was it round, as he believed? You could say he could discriminate between what was genuine truth and what was a lie. Ever have trouble with that? I once watched a bird who had gotten into a house and worked its way into a room with a large plate glass window. Sadly for the bird, it could not tell the difference between reality and illusion. How did I know? That bird kept flying into the window. That window was an illusion. It was a lie. After about a dozen whams against the glass, the bird gave up. It sat on the floor, unmoving and confused. That story illustrates another of the secret principles of life: *you must know the difference between truth and lies.*

Most of what the world is trying to teach you about conduct, attitude, and morality is a lie. Today's television, magazines, movies, and songs urge you to accept standards which Christians know are wrong. They want you to believe in a "flat" immoral world instead of God's glorious "round" one. How?

Well, they don't come right out and insist you live a lie. No. Like Satan in Genesis 3, they begin by denying God's eternal truth about life, people, conduct, standards, the future, home, values, and so many things. Then they urge you to conform. To them. They say it's harmless to smoke, drink, engage in premarital sex, have an abortion. They say everyone else is doing it. They say it won't hurt you or anyone else. They say they are right. They say you will find acceptability following their directions.

Placing yourself, including your social acceptability, into the hands of others is not very satisfying, especially if you know—deep in your heart—that they are wrong. You let them turn you into a Christopher Columbus sailing the wrong way. When you let the illusions of the world lead, you are overlooking God's clear warning about conforming to the world instead of transforming your mind to his newer and better ideals (Rom. 12:2). *Deciding to not conform to the world's value system* is another important secret principle of life.

The good old pickle jar

But how are we going to resist conforming? So much pressure! So hard to resist! Instead of trying to take on all the lies about everything wrong the world tells you, let me encourage *a "pickle jar" approach to resisting life's unsavory and deceitful pressures*. Think about the last time you opened a jar of pickles. Which was the hardest to get out? The first one, right? After the first one they pull out easily. Can you sense my application? The first time is the time to resist when the world tells you it's all right to lie, cheat, steal, hurt, or act sexually irresponsible. Doing wrong gets easier if you give in the first time. Recognize that fact and, as the ancient Romans warned one another, "resist the beginnings." That means you will have to say no to some things from the very first. You may even have to say no to one of your friends. Say it. Say it for your sake. Say it for their sake. If you need some help in doing that, go back to Chapter 6 and review the instructions on speaking and hearing, especially the part about sending a negative message. Think about this principle. Carefully.

The only thing we have to fear

Another one of life's secret principles has to do with the pressure we put on ourselves by our inner fear of failing, or of being proven wrong. Some people do very foolish things because they don't want to look "wrong." One young man I knew almost killed himself by drinking an entire bottle of whiskey because he said he could. He did and almost died. Another did kill himself proving he could leap off a second floor balcony. Nothing heroic there. Just dumb.

What's so wrong with failure? Making mistakes and committing errors are important to life. One important way we learn is through our mistakes. *Knowing that failure is not only common in life but crucial to it as well* is another of the secret principles. Once you get over the fear of failure the door opens to trying again, and again, and again until success crowns your effort. Thomas Edison experimented with more than a hundred filaments before he hit on the one that could make the light bulb beam—and keep on beaming. Treasure healthy failure. It's a lot more helpful than ignorant success. Recognize the fear of failing, or of being shown wrong, for what it is: concealment of any hope of success. You don't have to like to fail or enjoy making mistakes and looking dumb. Learn from it and don't let it happen twice. Especially, never risk your life, your health—or anyone else's—because you can't back down from a mistake in judgment. Admit you erred. Laugh at yourself. Learn.

Let's start putting things together

The "secret principles" I have mentioned so far in this chapter (and there are more coming) and the other ideas in this book are like pieces of a puzzle. We need to link them one to another if we hope to complete a stunning picture. How do you do that? How do you start?

If I were making a normal jigsaw puzzle I would pick out similar-looking border pieces, hook them together, and start my project by establishing the four sides. With the border completed I then would fill in the rest. When every piece is in its place the puzzle is done!

My advice for making everything fit is start with the border. That's better than grabbing pieces at random in the hope that two or more will mesh. If they do by chance, then what? You still don't have much to build on. Start with the border. And do I have good news for you: *your life has four sides.* You will live to your fullest potential when the four sides are properly linked. The subjects we discussed so far—communication, renegotiation, trust, and other living skills—develop in relationship to those four sides. In real life those four sides are equally important and can't be separated. But in our book we can take them apart and study them one by one.

Side one: your life context

The term *life context* covers a large area, as we said in Chapter 4. It includes your personal gifts, things like your singing ability, muscle coordination, mental capacity, problem-solving skills, artistic instinct, common sense, and other things. Those make up your unique life context. How important are they?

If your muscle coordination is poor and you don't have a steady hand, you will either need to develop those characteristics—or give up your desire to become a brain surgeon. If you discover that you have rhythm, but that you're tone deaf, you'll never make it as a musician. The talents you possess, or don't possess, affect the goals in life you can intelligently choose.

Other life-context considerations include things like where you live, the financial support system available to you, your physical size and strength, the kind of parental guidance you receive, the quality of your home life, and your education. Anything that directly affects your life choices is a part of your life context. If your parents have little money, you may not be able to attend Harvard. Availability of money is a part of your life context but that doesn't mean you can't get a good education at a local community college. But, if you still want to go to Harvard, get busy studying, use your intelligence, and work at getting a scholarship. If you weigh 220 pounds and can run like a deer, try for a football scholarship. All those considerations develop from your life context.

Your context also includes the things we noted earlier in the chapter: your moral values, your optimism or pessimism, your personality, the intensity of your desire to do things. All those, together, are "you" and affect the choices you can make.

Context and freedom

Your life context together with an acceptance and appreciation of your context are the springboard from which you dive into life. There you can claim that intriguing thing called *freedom*. People who claim freedom for themselves, and yet operate without any sense of context, aren't free at all. They are like a ship without an anchor. When the ocean is wide and the days are calm, the ship can usually (but not always) drift on and on. In a fierce storm, or when the ship is fighting heavy seas close to shore, the lack of an anchor is disastrous. A ship that is anchored can resist the pressures of ocean current, wind and tidal movement. It can hold its own. It's about the same with life. People who want to be free but forget their context are pushed around by whatever is the strongest pressure at any given moment.

True freedom is not the ability to flit about without any kind of restriction. If that were true, any piece of paper blown about by the March wind would be free. But that paper has no choice. Freedom, true freedom, includes choice. A solid life context sets the stage for choices. Without a solid context those choices evaporate. That's another of life's secret principles; *when you understand and control your context you get to make choices that are as close to freedom as a person can come.*

As a teenager I found out that I was unable to cheat in class. It's not that I was so pure. I couldn't cheat because everything in me seemed to resist it. In time I came to realize that I was really unable to cheat because I could not override the standards of conduct my parents practiced in their own lives and had taught me. My life context, a context that included my family's honor system, was tougher than any impulse to cheat.

Write out your context. All of it. You need to know your context, for it directly affects, even shapes, the decisions you are able to make. If your context needs improvement, go to it. *In reality you can affect your life context as much as it affects you.* That's another secret principle of life.

Side two just plain me

Every one of us will also have to factor our "me" into all our decisions. We are tied very tightly to our "me." Our "me" includes how we feel, what we want, the way we think. Those parts of my "me" shape my actions and decisions. One way of studying my "me" is by determining how well I accept responsibility.

Troubled people and people with a very low self-esteem (and don't forget the #1 concern of young people who wrote over the past dozen years is they don't like who they are) have difficulty accepting responsibility for their actions. They blame. Instead of accepting, they blame anyone they can. They are like their forefather Adam. Remember the story of when he hid when God came calling? When God asked Adam what he'd done, Adam skipped God's question and jumped to the blaming posture: "The woman you put here with me—she gave gave me some fruit from the tree, and I ate it" (Gen. 3:12). He accepted no part in the decision to disobey. Blame God. Blame Eve. He was not responsible. The truth is that he was hurting himself. He didn't take care of his "me."

People who accept responsibility for their action can be

described as having a good "I-position." We all need a solid I-position. Suppose you are asked by a friend to go someplace you don't really want to go. If your I-position is in good shape, you can simply say, "I can't go with you tonight." When pressed for more reasons, a person with a good I-position might answer, "I would be uncomfortable in a place like that." People with a solid I-position accept full responsibility for their decision. They don't pass blame on to anyone else.

A person with a very fragile I-position (or a nonexistent one) would fold and go, or beg off by blaming someone else saying, "My parents won't let me go there." Or he might plead sickness, saying, "I'd like to come but I'm feeling sick." The end result of both kinds of answers is the same. You don't go. But the second set of answers refuses personal responsibility and reflects a poor I-position.

I once counseled a girl who had a weak I-position. She told me a story of friends who were talking one day of good ways to shoplift. She did not want to shoplift. Her friends said they didn't want to shoplift either. All they wanted to do was talk about it. But talking led to deciding to look over a store to see if their ideas would work. She said she didn't want to go, but she went. Looking over the store they decided they would give shoplifting a try. Her reaction? You guessed it. Even though she said she didn't want to, she agreed to help. They were caught and taken to the police station. There she protested innocence and blamed the others. She insisted she had wanted no part of it. At her trial she tried to blame others again, but the judge wasn't swayed. He told her she had passed at least three opportunities to assert her I-position and avoid the whole mess. But she didn't. It took many hours of talking to her to help her begin to understand her problem. Her "me" was in real bad shape.

By contrast I remember another girl who was very different. She had no difficulty asserting her I-position, and accepting responsibility. She was out with her boyfriend when he said he wanted to drop in on a party. She told him she didn't want to go because it was not the kind of place she wished to be. When he insisted on going anyway, she told him that if he drove her there against her wishes, she'd call a taxi and go home. He didn't believe her and drove to the party. As soon as she arrived, she called a cab and left. She laid no blame on her boyfriend. He had his standards and she had hers. She took responsibility for her actions and asserted a solid I-position.

People who have a healthy I-position are easily recognizable. They say things like, "I see it this way . . ." or "I was thinking that . . ." or, "I believe it would be better if. . . ." Teenagers who talk that way have placed themselves squarely in the middle of any decision-making process. They accept the responsibility for what they might do to themselves or to others. They choose a course of action with which they can be comfortable and then they stick with it. They develop a lively and useful understanding of themselves and treat themselves as important people. Why do they feel this way? Because that's what they are! Take care of your "me." Only you can. Now why would that be a secret hidden to so many?

Side three: Your attitude toward others

John Donne wrote a poem more than 300 years ago that begins, "No man is an island. . . . " I'm sure you know of it. Even if you don't, it's true. No one stands alone. We are connected. Whatever we do affects others, and whatever others do affects us. Sometimes we may imagine we do things that will effect only ourselves. It doesn't work that way.

One afternoon a young girl who had been caught selling drugs was sent to talk with me. That's right. Sent. She didn't deny it. But she insisted that since she was affecting no one but herself her actions were no one else's business. I suggested we explore that statement. Was it true? Was she affecting only herself? We made a list of everyone who was affected by her action. In an hour's time we collected names of more than 90 individuals whose life pattern was in some way changed because of her action. Number 91 was me. I had wanted to play golf that afternoon, and instead I sat in the office with her. I didn't mind giving up my golf, but I couldn't tolerate that line of "I'm-hurting-no-one-but-myself."

Our actions always affect other people. Everything we do and everything we say affects our world whatever its size. In return, people affect us. Just think of your class at school. Isn't it true that when your class cut-up gets bored his actions stop the educational process for everyone? Tired of learning, or yearning for attention, he creates an atmosphere that just plugs the educational moment. You may laugh at his antics, but two things are for sure: (1) he's in charge, and (2) you aren't learning anything.

That's a negative example. There are also many positive ones. Can you think of a time when you and/or your friends changed a person? Think. Or, was there a time when you saw one person's actions affect the whole group—positively? Ever seen someone stand up to a group and firmly assert that what he or she believes is right, no matter what others say? And haven't you seen an entire group change as a result? I have. Those are the kinds of people you want to affect you. They don't manipulate. They model. Then it's up to you to decide your action pattern.

All of us need to be models and to have models. Keeping a balance between these two possibilities is crucial to successfully practicing the art of living. Those who always let others take the lead and determine what will happen are just as lopsided as those who must always have their way. Find the golden mean, the middle ground. When someone is sending out the right signals, you follow. But when someone is pushing too hard, take the initiative! Send out a triple-E message!

Triple-E messages

Triple-E messages are "lay off it" warnings. Triple-E messages emphasize *the event, the effect,* and *the emotion.* Confusing? Here's how they work.

A friend of mine sent a triple-E message to his pal not long ago. His pal had the habit of dominating every situation he was in. He was loud. His abrasive voice hurt your ears. My friend put a pleasant stop to it. He said to his pal, "Your voice is so loud that it hurts my ears, and I don't like it." That was his triple-E message.

See how it works? The *event*—a loud voice. The *effect*—it hurt his ears. The *emotion*—he didn't like it. And how did his pal respond? "I didn't know that!" From then on he made a conscious effort to speak less emphatically and in softer tones.

Send triple-E messages. They are OK. Triple-E messages help you live responsibly with others. They are a useful response to anyone trying to dominate your life. Don't fire them off all the time. Use them selectively—like when your mother insists on telling you how to fix your hair. Instead of griping and storming out the door why don't you send her a gentle triple-E message? Try saying, "Mother, let me choose my own hair style. I know what's right for kids today. I feel stupid when you don't even trust me to decide how to cut my hair." Or you might say to a teacher, "Mrs. Barnes, I can select my own book for the book reports. I know what to choose. It will help me develop confidence in my capacity to make a judgment."

Just so things don't get lopsided in your mind, always remember the positive side in your relationship with others. Not everyone trying to make a suggestion wants to take over your life. Sometimes friends are just offering helpful advice. You need to receive it. Right? We have said that you learned most of the things you know by both experience and by the insights and observations others have shared with you. You have helped others, too. Keep contact—for the sake of both of you. But always be sensitive to your I-position, to the three Es, and to your own sense of self-esteem as you relate to others. Those are some of those secret principles.

Side four: a right relationship with God

In black and white, side four looks so bland. But this is the most important element of the basic four. If you aren't right with God nothing works. Be sure you understand the relationships—God's with you and yours with God. Start where it all started to begin with: God's relationship with you.

Your loving God has put an unbelievably high value on you. You are more valuable than his Son. That must be so. The possibility of an eternity without you in his heaven was so unacceptable to him that he set salvation's plan in motion. "For God so loved the world that he gave his one and only Son . . . " (John 3:16). He did it for you. More than that, he didn't want you left alone on his earth. Right? Wasn't it God who said, "It is not good for the man to be alone"? (Gen. 2:18). God then completed his human creation with a life companion complementary to the man. He made woman for man and man for woman. He gave them to each other. That was not only God's way of saying that marriage is important. It was also his way of saying that all relationships to all others are important.

It's clear in God's Word that from the dawn of history God has been surrounding his many children with other people, with other experiences and other elements of creation to make life worth living. God has even set the standards for how we relate to all that is created whether animate or inanimate. These standards for stewardship of all he has made are intended to bring us joy, satisfaction, and the full life. When we live in a balanced awareness of God's intent, the practice of these same standards not only brings joy to us, but to others, as well.

As a final blessing, God gives us himself in the person of the Holy Spirit. That Spirit comes to us through God's own means, the Bible, prayer, Baptism, and the Lord's Supper, bringing us power to live a sensitive, interrelated life with brothers and sisters in t*His* world as we also ready ourselves to live in the world to come.

Knowing and believing all that I have written in these last few paragraphs is the fourth bordering side of life. Not knowing what this section contains, or not believing it, makes for an incomplete existence. We'll share a bit more about that one in Chapter 9.

People who are in balance

Knowing that there are four sides to your life is important, but it isn't all you need to know. A man I know is extremely active in church. He prays often in private and in public. He studies the Bible. But, sad to say, he ignores his home and the needs of his wife and children. Actually, he ignores almost everyone else with his single-minded devotion to God. That's not good. That's not what God intends. His life is warped. It's not warped because he is devoted to God. It's warped because he has ignored the three other God-given bordering areas in life. He has forgotten his context, passed over his responsibility to other people, and has not developed a proper commitment to himself. Somehow you also need to keep the four areas in healthy tension and balance. If one side is emphasized too much, or if another side is neglected, you cannot live a full life. Things must be kept in balance.

Keeping things in balance won't automatically solve all life's problems, but it's the place to start. A balanced, four-sided life expects success at problem solving. However, to successfully solve problems you also must have a proven problem-solving process. Do you have one? If you do, good. Keep it. But also compare it with the one I will present. Then integrate the best of both. You see, that's another of life's secret principles: *you need a good problem-solving process in order to get good results.*

Problem solving

Problems (everyone has them) are a problem. But problem solving doesn't have to be. The best approach to the problem of problems is a good problem-solving process. Take a look at this six-step approach:

1. define the problem;
2. consider various solutions;
3. choose one;
4. implement it;
5. evaluate it and, if necessary,
6. change by going back and starting again.

Using this problem-solving process the problem of problems diminishes—unless you skip some of the steps. For example, you must identify the problem. To test how well you understand that point consider this real-life problem.

You ask your dad for the car but he refuses to let you have it. So what's the problem? It could be: (a) you haven't resolved a long-term struggle between you and your dad about who will make decisions in your life; or (b) you now must figure out how to tell your date that you'll have to double with a couple she doesn't like; or (c) how will you handle a sense of rejection that leaves you feeling you are still a kid with no brains; or (d) the car needs some new tires, but your dad hasn't time to take it to the service station. Which of those four possibilities is the problem? You must identify the problem before any good solution will start surfacing.

Sometimes the solutions we come upon (the very proper solutions) are so painful and unacceptable that we feel we can't use them. But that's something else entirely. Another problem? Bottom line: be sure to define the problem. Nothing happens until you do. Nothing helpful, anyway. Then go for the solutions (plural).

Suppose this is the problem: You are being hassled at home. Most of the hassling stems from your poor grades. For the moment let's accept this as a proper definition of your problem. Now let's turn to solutions. Think about it for a minute. What kind of solutions might be available? I can offer at least four. One, you could study more. Two, you could get help from someone. Three, you could cheat. Four, you could quit school. Before we pick a solution, let's weigh each of them.

Is number one helpful? Could you study more? If you don't understand what's going on now, will more study help you? Not much help there! So turn to solution number two. How about asking for help? That might work, if you know someone who can give you the help you need. If your problem is the metric system and your father doesn't know any more about it than you do, you won't make much progress by asking him for help! Turn to number three: cheat. Maybe you're like me, and can't. Maybe no one who sits around you knows any more about it than you do and so you can't cheat. You turn to solution number four. Why not quit school? If you quit school what's going to happen to your ambition to become an airline pilot? You can't be a flyer and flunk math! We've run through them all. Which has the most possibilities? Number two?

Suppose you focus on two, but instead of asking your dad for help you ask a friend. In deciding to look for help from a friend you have taken steps 3 and 4 in our problem-solving process: you have *chosen* a solution and *implemented* it. You ask him for the help and he agrees. What's next? Weeks pass. You evaluate your solution (Step 5) and find (sad to say) that your friend knows only a little more about math than you. Time to reevaluate (Step 6). It's obvious. You will need several friends to help! Ask them. Problem solved. In time you become so skilled that you don't need help anymore. Everything is great. Why? You used a problem-solving process.

If you take the time to measure your problems against this six-step solution technique you will not only identify and solve the problems you will also improve the quality of your life. You may even want to become a professional problem-solver!

The happiness question

One more part of life's secret principles: *you must know how to deal with "the happiness question."* By "the happiness question," I refer to the common belief that the goal of every life should be happiness. Remember those fairy stories that all end: ". . . and they lived happily ever after"? I don't believe that's a very useful goal. And I don't think it's very real in your life. If you accept the premise that things which bring unhappiness are bad, and things which bring happiness are good, your approach to life will be affected significantly. I don't accept that premise.

I question whether happiness is the highest and finest goal for life. Setbacks, defeats, unattained objectives, impossible dreams, and unfulfilled yearnings are very important to shaping a fulfilling existence. Those supposedly negative things are important to you—in the same way that pain is useful. Through pain we recognize that something in our body needs attention! Pain, or its location, can give us a good idea of the problem. Doesn't the doctor ask you, "Where does it hurt—and how much?" When you don't hurt at all you are either totally healthy—or dead. The absence of pain means either that everything is fine, or that you are out of it entirely. Pain, in proper amounts, prevents the development of many more serious problems. Unhappiness can be just as useful as pain.

The Bible doesn't say much about what we call happiness. It uses words like contentment, commitment, faith, joy and trust, but not much about happiness. Why? Is it because the goal of happiness is not from God, but maybe from some other source? Could it be that happiness, as a dominant goal, tends to make us compromise ourselves—to our own hurt? Instead of making happiness a goal, we may need a goal of making a distinction between what is a horrendous disaster and something that is only a temporary irritation. Let me explain.

Suppose you are a football player in a big game. Near the end of the first half you are blind-sided and knocked cold. The coach keeps you out for the second half. Is that bad? Is that a disaster? Is that the end of happiness for you? It depends. Missing a chance to play in the big game may be irritating and disturbing, but playing football with a concussion, or making a costly error because of your confusion is worse. Some people don't know the difference between disaster and irritation. When they don't get what they want it is "bad." Maybe. But maybe not. Consider these helpful words from the apostle Paul: "We know that in all things God works for the good of those who love him" (Rom. 8:28). That verse helps me with the happiness question.

Paul does not say that all things are good. Tragic things do happen to people. It is tragic when someone is injured or killed in an automobile accident. It is tragic when a mother dies of cancer or when people are fired unjustly from their jobs. The Bible tells such tragic stories. The classic is the story of Joseph. He was sold into slavery by his brothers and separated for years from his father. No happiness there. Pure tragedy! But the story doesn't end there. In time he became the second most powerful man in Egypt. From that position he was later able to save his whole family from starvation. When he looked back on the many "bad" things that had happened to him, he told his brothers, "You intended to harm me, but God intended it for good" (Gen. 50:20). Tragedies are not always tragic! Never factor God out of the things that happen. He is right there, in the middle of all the events in your life. He is fully capable of turning the most grievous personal pain into a blessing. Knowing and believing that, you can confront the happiness question. And you will know another of life's secret principles: *things aren't always what they seem.*

Putting it all together

With a load of effort, a lot of prayer, and a mountain of trust in God, you can apply the many secret principles we have talked about in this chapter to your life. They will make a tremendous difference in the way you live. These secret principles will not make things easier for you. Just better! The "growing" we studied in the life of Christ is not easy! These secret principles will open to you the good and positive alternatives God has provided to every event, every question, every opportunity of life. You have choices! Make them. Plant your feet on the road which, blessed by the Spirit, leads to the full life in Christ. It's a great road, worth the walking. One of the best parts of walking on that road is that you can do so with a positive sense of Christ's presence. He is always there. Because he is always there, you will discover you can expect good things (his kind of good things) in your every tomorrow. There's nothing secret about that!

Now it's on to another area where the secret principles work. Pack them up. Bring them along. Let's get going. Time's awastin'. There's life out there to be loved and lived!

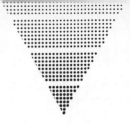

Eight

LIFE AND SEXUALITY—
TWO OF GOD'S GIFTS

I wrote no special chapter on life and sexuality in this book's first edition. It's not that people weren't concerned about life in the 1970s (they were), or that they didn't care about sex (they did). But the public attitude toward both was different. Life was more precious and less threatened, or so it appeared. Teenage suicide and some varieties of youthful self-abuse were not a national concern. Nor were our public attitudes toward sex so loose that teen pregnancies and sexual promiscuousness were a conspicuous and continuous reality. Moreover, we were not assaulted by distorted, abusive, and easily available sex at every turn. Add it up: there was less *mis*information.

I can almost hear some of you say, "Less *mis*information today? Compared to a dozen years ago? You've got to be kidding!" But I'm not. Not at all.

While it's true that some kinds of basic information about human sexuality (more often than not, it's little more than pictures about human plumbing) and the vivid portrayals of sexual practices (the sweaty I-gotta-have-it-now TV/movie dramas) are more common today, that's not the whole of it. It's not even a substantial half of it. There's more to basic sexual information than that! The truth is missing: the real truth about our sexuality and of God's sexual intention for us! That truth has been mangled beyond recognition via TV's soap operas and dramas, and Hollywood's movie distortions. There's nothing really informative about all those! They are *mis*informative. They tell so little that's true about our sexuality and what's finest in our sexual relations that their portrayals are little more than cartoons of God's beautiful intent. Need I mention the weird books, the odd magazines, the true "confessions," the wickedly confused and confusing songs, or the sick lives of any number of brassy, proud national figures? The apostle Paul's evaluation of 2000 years ago is true again today: "They exchanged the truth of God for a lie, and worshiped and served created things rather than the Creator. . . . God gave them over to shameful lusts" (Rom. 1:25-26). Now *that's* the truth.

I first sensed that all this flip-flopping of the truth was happening when, in the early 1980s, specific questions about the world's ideas of sex began arriving in my mail and surfacing at youth conferences. The initial trickle has become a steady stream. It's obvious: many young men and women are confused—Christians, too—about sexual right and wrong, and they know it. More than that, they are looking for help. Others know what's right and wrong but feel like they are waging a lonely battle on behalf of truth. And they are getting tired.

As questions about sexuality multiplied, companion questions about drugs (including alcohol, a nationally recognized drug) and pessimistic comments about the value of life began cropping up. I am convinced all these concerns—sex, drugs, suicide—are connected. While each has specific characteristics and all require widely differing responses they have at least this in common: the best and most helpful approach to all of them begin with an individual's understanding of God and of his finest intention for us.

In this chapter I want to confront these concerns as directly and honestly as I know how. I will give the best answers I know to the most common questions I have received from teens about dating, sexual intercourse, masturbation, drugs, suicide, and other equally important concerns. There are few one-line answers. These subjects are not that simple. But it will be the truth, and nothing but the truth.

It's all connected

I am assuming you have read everything in this book up to here. This isn't the chapter with which to start. It's all connected. By reading, and keeping in mind, all that has come before, you now know that expressions of your humanity, whether positive or negative, are part of your context. Remember that from Chapter 7? One element of your context is your understanding of God. Do you believe that everything God made is good? Everything? Including sunrises, summer, strawberry sundaes, *and* sex. Do you? I do.

God made it all good. If, now, someone bloats themselves on sundaes, or blinds themselves with sunrises, or burns themselves in the summer sun, does that mean the sundae, the sunrise, or the summer is bad? Of course not. Same for sex. So start with this; sex was created good by a good God and it was intended to stay that way. It is still good *when seen and understood in the divine context*. That divine context includes recognizing our sexuality *before marriage* and our sexuality *after marriage*. They are two different things. Both were created good. Under God's blessing they still are good. Both are within God's intention for his children. But they are different from each other.

Just so there is no misunderstanding: God's "before marriage" intention for our sexuality does not include sexual intercourse. It does include developing the skills, understanding, and sensitivities you will need for positive, lifelong relationships with others, male and female. Our *before marriage* sexuality encourages us to date, to dance, to meet with those of the opposite sex even when the thought of those experiences scare us. There are inner sexual warmings (likely to become the "burning" the apostle Paul talks about in 1 Corinthians 7:9 that later makes us want to marry) that help good social outreach happen. Those warm stirrings mean we need to prepare ourselves for responsible life relationships with others. All that preparation comes long before the time for *after marriage* sexual intercourse. Our *before marriage* sexuality adds richness to that later climax. True.

Moreover, our *before marriage*—and always developing—sexuality pushes us toward the "feelings" dimensions of life. Feelings are important gifts of God. They are as important to life as taste buds. They make us think, reflect, and finally act. Feelings are one of life's energizers. Continually hiding your feelings, or denying that you have feelings, are rejections of part of God's creative intent. You are supposed to have feelings. But feelings must be controlled. They must not control you. To control them they must be understood, too. Learning how to understand and control feelings is another of those teenage "growing" tasks which Jesus experienced.

Some more. Our developing sexual senses press us to develop self-control, a very important part of later marital relations, sexual and otherwise. Learning to control yourself (that's not to be confused with stunting important and authentic inner drives) will make you a better husband or wife *and* a better person. You aren't ready for a full-blown commitment to another person until you have developed the kind of control that intentionally and consciously directs your energies.

If you ignore the truth in the preceding paragraphs about *before marriage* sexuality, and become sexually active, even though you are not fully ready, two things will happen: (1) you will have pitted yourself against God (in the Bible God is clear about his anger toward sexual activity between those who are unmarried and calls it a sin); and (2) you will come to know you are a people-user, willing to use another person when your inner "burning" requires it. Both of those discoveries spell trouble.

Even as I tell you how vigorously God opposes *before marriage* intercourse I want also to assure you God can forgive that sin also. When you truly confess any sin and ask for forgiveness, God gives it to you. In the forgiving he also gives you a new and changed mind to help you resist what you know is wrong. He will help you resist. Not only is that good news, it puts the finger on what will always be your real problem: the human consequences of what you have done. God forgives, but there are human consequences which come, also, to forgiven sinners. They are the tragic aftermath of even forgiven sins.

Like? The least problem you may develop from *before marriage* sexual intercourse is an unwanted pregnancy. The least. But even that "least" presses some difficult decisions on you. For example, when the child is born as the result of *before marriage* sexual relations there will be certain specific, lifelong responsibilities you will face, ready or not! Your baby will not only need a new pair of shoes, but a lot of other things as well. Who's to provide all that? Your folks? Welfare? You? Whether, when, and how (even if) you pursue a career will have to be considered. Your little child is no Barbie doll to be played with for a while and then reboxed for later fun. That baby wants and needs lots of help. Right now. Giving that help is your responsibility.

Should you, instead of keeping and rearing the child, decide to place the child for adoption, you will often think of him or her over the years, wondering—and wishing—and hoping. Sad. Almost the worst fate is to have the child, keep it, *and then hate it* for what she or he supposedly did to you. Did to you? That's not what happened. *You* were the "doer."

No, I didn't forget the other choice. I wish I could. Abortion. Should you make that bad decision you will live with a lifelong realization that you took your child's life. Say it like it is: your child's life was taken. By you. I can't make it come out any different. No amount of explanation will change the truth. Please understand that. And don't muddy the water by long debates about aborting pregnancies that are the result of rape or incest. That's not the subject. The subject is people who have *before marriage* sexual intercourse and then solve the "problem" of a resultant pregnancy through abortion. Bad news.

Just so we get *all* the real truth on the table, those who have *before marriage* sexual intercourse must face the possibility of contracting herpes, syphilis, gonorrhea, AIDS, and quite an additional catalog of frightening treatable and untreatable diseases. And scary as all that is, we haven't yet mentioned the psychological, social, and familial aspects of *before marriage* sexual intercourse, with or without a resulting pregnancy. Like "the morning after." After having *before marriage* sexual intercourse, many reject the very person with whom they earlier "made love." That's nothing new. It's old as the Bible. Read about Amnon who seduced his sister Tamar. After their sexual adventure, we are told ". . . he hated her more than he had loved her" (2 Sam. 13:15).

As frightening as my comments of the past few paragraphs may be, fear is not my intention. I wrote what I did so that you would be fully informed. I have shared nothing new. It's all written in history, written in Scripture, written in literature, written in professional's case studies, written with tears in silence. You have the right—and a need—to know the truth.

Those other problem words: <u>adultery</u> *and* <u>abuse</u>

Just to complete the picture, please understand that God has very specific ideas about what's proper about *after marriage* sexual relationships, too. One of the Ten Commandments specifically addresses one kind of improper sexual relationship even after marriage. The words, "You shall not commit adultery" refer to sexual intercourse when one or both of those involved is already married, but to someone else. The marriage agreement is then adulterated, flawed, stained, marred. That is a sin. God is as angry about that kind of disobedience as *before marriage* sexual intercourse. Adultery damages commitment, hurts people, and changes the beauty of *after marriage* sexual intercourse into selfish lust. That sounds a lot different than the way the world tries to portray it. Right?

Even when the sexual intercourse is between two who are married to each other, the marriage bond never permits any physical or psychological abuse of one's partner, or any other warping of proper husband-wife relationships which movies, dramas, and books portray as acceptable. When a woman is sexually demeaned by her partner or a man sexually debased by what he is asked to do, God is not pleased and there will not be a blessing on their marriage.

There's a lot more that can and must be said about the sexual relationships in marriage. The positive needs accenting: its beauty, its excitement, its power to please and fulfill, its divine origin. But I'm not going to say more here. Those many good things that must be presented and treasured belong in another book, with another audience in mind. I want to keep you—my unmarried, but very sexually aware, teenage friend—in the forefront. There's time enough to deal with that other world of awe and wonder. Right now we need to work together on shaping your sexuality during your exciting and awesome *before marriage* years.

Let's start with dating

My dad was a salesman. He would tell me, "Nothing happens in the business world until someone sells something." For him the whole world of economics was simple; it all starts with a sale. What the salesman has sold, the manufacturer then makes, the shipper ships, and the buyer receives. My dad's view won't bear too much testing. But a seed of truth is there.

Dating is like selling. In the same way that selling makes

industry's wheels turn, your decision to date starts your inner wheels turning toward adult sexual maturity. If it doesn't start there it begins somewhere very close. And a decision to date means boyfriends and girlfriends.

Moms and dads say *boy*friends and *girl*friends. Ditto for those in the later teens. But in the earliest teens you say "boy*friends*" and "girl*friends.*" Listen for that difference in accent. It's there. The shifting accent reminds us that relationships which later become more sexual begin as social experiences. All you seek at first is a sexually opposite friend. Why? A sexually opposite friend sees things different than you and from another perspective introduces rich detail to your life. Hooray for the difference! Hooray for all the details!

The first moves between sexually opposite teens are very cautious. Recall the last 6th or 7th grade dance you attended? Where were the boys—and where were the girls? Most boys with boys? And girls with girls? That's normal. The earliest teen years are a cautious, testing time. To see it even more clearly, check out what's happening outside the school when classes are over. See all those first "moves"; the laughing, the teasing, the talking, the outrageous good humor, the exaggerated behavior. What does it mean? It means it's dating time—or nearly so!

Some of the first notes I get from 6th and 7th grade guys ask, "How do you ask a girl to dance?" Don't think those notes have anything to do with dancing. Not really. They have to do with: (1) how to handle rejection, or its possibility, and (2) how to make those first social moves. Like some suggestions? Be direct. Smile. Compliment. If you don't know how to dance say, "It would be so much fun to dance, especially with you. Would you teach me?" What's to lose? These are the earliest moves in dating. It's natural to want to date. It's just as natural to be nervous about it. But you can do it!

First dates usually work out best in groups. Double date. Triple date. Talking happens easier that way. Lots of others are around. You also get to see the way others handle themselves. Don't forget to be involved. No silent observers. And don't forget to help others get involved as well. Ask questions. Laugh at answers. Avoid always "showing up" others. Be a pal.

How old before you date? That's not easy to answer. Take a look around. What are others doing? The best answer has a lot to do with what's going on in your corner of the world. Don't try to be the first. Move into the dating world at a speed you feel is comfortable. Keep in mind that dating is only one of the worlds you are exploring in the teen years. There are intellectual and physical and psychological and spiritual realms, as well. They all need attention. All. But in this chapter the spotlight is on one: your social, sexually maturing self.

Oh yes, one thing more. Date those your age. It helps you see how things work out with others like you and prepares you for tomorrow. When you date a much older person, you are either getting in over your head or they are not challenging themselves. Ever wonder why not? Could it be they can't handle someone their own age? Think about it.

Going together—or at least thinking about it

It's probable that in the process of dating you will find yourself drawn to one—or two—of your opposite sex friends more than others. You may also sense that someone is being drawn to you. It feels like a magnetic force-field! Someone is positive and someone negative and attracting is high energy stuff. Most of us like that. It's nice being noticed in a special way. It makes you feel good. It may really narrow down and you may sense a desire for a kind of exclusiveness in your relationship. And if you don't feel that way it could be your "friend" who tilts that direction. What's that all about?

That process of deepening feelings and attaching yourself to another in a special way has many names. One that most people understand and use is "going together."

Going together has been around for a long time. It is not necessarily good—or inevitably bad. It depends on you and how you handle it. Let me share some things about going together that other teens have told me.

Teens tell me that a potentially "bad thing" about going together is that it limits your contact with other people whether they are male or female. That's a fact. Those going together know fewer people. Those you do know you will not know as well. Why? It's largely a "time" question. When you go together there's not enough time to keep up other friendships or develop new ones. And there is usually too much exclusiveness in a going-together relationship—you really don't want to know others. That's one reason going together usually belongs in the later part of your life—*after* you have met lots of different people, developed a broader understanding of social interaction, and refined your catalog of acceptable choices. Reinforcing this is a generally accepted understanding that you develop your personality through the people you meet. This means the more you meet, the better your chances for developing into the fullest (and most attractive) human being you can be. The fewer you meet, the more you limit your potential. Make sense?

Of course there's another side. A "good" (and sometimes important) benefit of going together is that you have date insurance. You don't have to finagle a way to attend the prom or fuss around figuring out how to get to the Saturday night movies. Any other benefits you can develop? Think about them. Consider the pros and cons. Weigh them. Do it carefully. Look out for yourself . . . and others.

After you gather and organize data about going together you can move on to deciding whether it will be good (does your ego need a little "going-together" reinforcement) or bad (aren't confident enough to risk new relationships?) for you to go together. In the process you must also confront and consider two big dating and going-together realities: love and intimacy.

Where friendship can end and trouble begin

Look out for the four-letter words. Though they are not all "bad," it seems to me that all have a tendency to inflame! Like *love*, for instance. Love is a four letter word and a powerful one. But look out! It can turn things around in the wink of an eye.

One fascinating thing about love is that it is not dictionary defined. Is it definable? Try to accurately capture its flavor with words. Lots have. Love is a word that is best described—understood—through actions. That's what makes it both so beautiful, so powerful, and so potentially dangerous. The beauty is that you act out your deepest sensitivities. Others react in kind. The power is that it breaks down resistance, stirs up response, scales emotional heights. The danger is that it can make negative actions look like positive reactions.

If it's that dynamic, can it ever be said that a teenager is in love? Real love? I get lots of letters asking that. My answer? Of course they can and often are. Teenage love is real, as real as love at any age. Even if some call it "puppy love" (insinuating that it shouldn't be taken seriously), the energy is there. If it must be called something different, I prefer to call it "first love."

It's true that you can "get over" your first love. Most of us do. But it's just as true that you can get over your third, fourth, and fifth love, as many have done! If that weren't true widows and widowers would never remarry in the name of love and live out another pleasing and satisfying relationship! Mark teen love down as real love and treat it with love-ing tenderness. That's the truth, but it's also the seed bed of a problem: intimacy.

By the very nature of love, it is always moving toward increased intimacies. Not just sexual intimacy. It moves toward intimacy of every kind. Intimate moments. Intimate thoughts. Intimate words. Intimate experiences. Intimate hopes. Intimate dreams. If it's true love how intimate should it become?

That depends. The boundary of intimacy, whether verbal or physical, must be limited to your context—not by what you want, or even yearn, to do. That's probably quite apparent to you and your loved one. I'm thinking about what you have the position in life and the preparation to do. All of that. Let *all* of that determine how intimate you become.

In the meantime stay away from private discussions which you cannot do anything about, like the deep feelings your "friend" may have toward his or her parents; reflections on an early life experience which has left a scar; career decisions which are actually none of your business. As you love your friend, remember that you are not a trained counselor. Don't explore private moments in their life. You have no right or expertise. If you wouldn't do experimental surgery on another's body, don't attempt experimental manipulation of their mind. Watch what you say. Don't presume a mental or emotional intimacy which doesn't really exist.

What's true of the mind of another is equally true of his or her body. You have no right to explore another's body, certainly not in the name of love! I can't tell you what is absolutely appropriate or absolutely inappropriate on the subject of bodily contact, but there do appear to be some sensible principles. Start with this one which I first heard from Charlie Shedd. He suggests that one boundary of bodily contact should be clothes. If the part of the body you are about to explore is normally covered by clothing, leave it alone. Covered things ought to stay that way and shouldn't be touched. How's that for a specific and clear suggestion? Make sense? I think so.

He would suggest sensible principle two: there's something fiery and supersexual about skin touching skin. That's the way God intended it to be. In the *after marriage* sexual contact, intimate touching is his created way of preparing those already committed through marriage for a climaxing sexual intercourse. The sexual intercourse that intimate touching energizes is an exciting *after marriage* expression of love that builds families, establishes caring homes, and makes for pleasing and godly memories. Intimate touching fits in that framework. Just like you wouldn't rev up a car, drop it in first gear and take off in a garage, don't rev up your intimacy responses when there's no place to go that won't end up troubling you or the one you say you love.

So what is acceptable intimacy? It's easier for you to answer that than for me. I mean, you know what stirs you just right and what stirs you too much. I always enjoyed hand holding . . . and obviously so do others. I find a kiss very pleasing. Do you? I liked (and like) sitting close, talking low, laughing together a lot. Sound dumb? Lovers know that's not true! Activities like skating, walking, dancing, and many other very important but less volatile sharings are nice. They build. They build you. They build others. They are like layers of lacquer covering a relationship of love. Each new and different sharing adds sheen and depth.

But don't try to achieve that gorgeous glossy effect by slapping on globs of lacquer all at one time. The results would be a mess. Intimacy is like that, too. Warm up a little at a time as the relationship deepens and as the possibilities of commitment increase. Time is always on your side. No hurry. In general take the advice of the mayonnaise jar: "Keep cool but don't freeze."

Why not be one of life's winners?

When it comes right down to it there are not a lot of rules or specific directions which God has given to govern our social/sexual conduct. Instead of pages of specific rules, he establishes human values and gives us specific beliefs. Those are no small thing! Values and beliefs are like commanders of the mind. They can control. They are able to help or hinder. Through those of us who have these twin gifts God influences his creation. Those whose God-given values and beliefs are strong bring blessing to themselves and others. They are winners in life. Life is a joy to them. They support their friends and are usually supported in return. Those whose values and beliefs are weak are usually a burden for they are never quite sure what to do—unless it's the next impulsive thing that comes to mind.

But what specific values and attitudes do winners have that set them aside as someone special and that help them deal with issues, like sex, so much more positively?

There have been any number of clinical studies developed that seek to identify the basic characteristics of life's winners. Based on those studies, your authors' experiences, and biblical insights a number of "winner" characteristics surface. Check them out. Are they correct? Do you agree? Where do you fit?

First, winners believe in something. If you ask them what it is, they will tell you. Illinois' 1987 Miss Teenage, Diane Shirley, made a stirring confession of Christian and personal faith as she prepared to go to the national competition in Hawaii. As she spoke it was obvious that she knew Christ. She also knew herself and her values. She was not confused about either. How did she get such a strong faith? Like everyone else who is faith-full, it came from God, from parents, from friends, from prayer, from study. She knows (all Christians know) that God has a will and a plan for her. The same is true for you. Ask God to make you faith-full. He will. He promises.

Second, winners have goals. They have a direction for life; a commitment. All a commitment really means is that you have taken an intentional position in your world and have adopted an active stance toward life. Winners have done this. They are involved. No sideline living for them. No aimless floating. No letting another make key decisions. Winners do more than react—they respond.

Third, winners also have an attitude of loving care toward themselves and others. People are valuable to them, whether it's me-people or you-people. No one is there to be used. They won't do it to others and they can't let others do it to them. People are to be loved and served, not used. That's point three.

Remember the other two? Faith-full. Actively committed to goals. Can you begin to see how all this can be tied into a useful view of sex and your sexuality?

Fourth: winners are willing to take responsibility for their actions and even their experiences. M. Scott Peck in his book *The Road Less Traveled* points out that while all human beings have trouble with accepting responsibility (remember Adam and Eve's struggle with that in the garden?) the really sick people have a lot more trouble with it. He says that *neurotics* get in trouble by taking responsibility for everything (too much) and *psychopaths* get in trouble by taking responsibility for nothing (too little). Winners know what, and how much, responsibility is theirs. They identify it and claim it.

For example, winners know they can influence others and affect the outcome of things. For that reason they actively and openly make their wishes known, all the while being ready to accept the consequence of their decision. Things don't always work as they planned. That's how winners also learn how to deal with failure and develop the ability to seek and accept both divine and human forgiveness.

Fifth, winners know there are outcomes—results—to all that they do. Sometimes things turn out as they intended and hoped. They take satisfaction and pleasure in those results. And when they fail? Winners learn from their mistakes. Winners know that as far as the future is concerned a valuable lesson learned from a failure is as useful as a valuable lesson learned from a success.

Sixth; one other insight that large-scale studies and personal observations teach: winners know the difference between what's real and true in life and what's unreal and untrue. (More specifics on that will come in Chapter 9.) While they realize that they are subjected to incredible pressures on all sides, winners cut through the unreal to the real. How? They search for God's way. It's there, clearly presented in Scripture. They pattern themselves after the best of this world who live by the highest standards. They seek God's presence in their life however they can find it. They search for Christian friends and keep company with God's people of highest quality. They trust their judgment and use their head and say intelligent things like, "If it doesn't make sense, it doesn't make sense." No wonder they are winners.

Things that do make sense

Winners know things that make sense? Like what? Name something. Sure. How about this: sex is a choice. Sexual intimacy doesn't just "happen" to you. You are not hopelessly swept into sexual relations like a piece of bark on a raging river. You are not without controls. Not unless it is rape. Losers act like key decisions in life are out of their control. They say, "I *fell* in love," and mean it! For them it's like tripping over something. Right? And when they think a relationship is over don't losers say, "I *lost* my feelings for . . ." as if it happened overnight *to* them? I'm always tempted to say, "Well, let's go see if we can't find your feelings! Maybe you dropped them in the parking lot. Could they be in the lost and found?" Losers get snared with that kind of talk. Not winners. Winners know sex (and a lot of other important things) is a choice. So how do you chose?

A person chooses by applying their congruence. Remember congruence? Congruence is the meshing of your inner person (your thoughts, values, morals) with your outer person (your actions). All the choices you make in life flow out of an application of your congruence. Based on congruence you will decide (it's all fairly final—decide means "to cut") which choices you will make. Let me show you how it works.

Before sexual intercourse takes place, a lot of decisions based on congruence have already been made. The accumulation of those individual decisions sets the stage for whatever finally happens. Like who you will go out with, how your relationship has developed, what kind of touchings have been allowed, where you actually go. Did you decide against a double date? Did you decide to be alone . . . and where? What kind of inner attitude toward *before marriage* sexual intercourse have you determined upon? See how the deciding works? I'll bet the opinion of your parents, of your friends, and of your community are in there somewhere, too. When you add up the early decisions, the last one is no surprise. Make your decisions make sense. Make them make sense to you. Develop and maintain your congruence.

Is the answer no ever positive?

Nancy Reagan popularized saying no, but she didn't invent it. When we are tempted to take drugs she advises us all, "Just say no." God advised Eve in the same way years earlier. All of us must learn how to say it. No. We will be tempted. We will be tested. We will be tried. Under temptation, or trial, or test, the correct answer is often no. Just that simple. No.

That answer is positive and helpful, especially when someone you care about wants you to do what you congruently know is wrong. When that moment comes the response is no.

Not sure you can say it? A lovely young lady in California told me how to send a no-message that is emphatic but still tender. She said that when no must be the answer say, "I can't do that. It wouldn't be right for me." No ranting. No name calling. A direct and courageous claiming of the right. A clear-cut rejection of the wrong. Super communication. A tremendous triple-E message. What a great way to tell a friend no. Solid futures get built on that kind of answer. It's a positive no.

If the invitation comes with intimidation and pressure or force, don't cringe or waffle. Let your response be a loud and direct: "No." Join Joseph. In the face of dangerous temptation he said, "How then could I do such a wicked thing and sin against God?" (Gen. 39:9). He got everything important into his answer, and in the right order. Get your answer out, then get out of there. Most of the need for "no-ing" in life seems to surface in the dark corners of life while you are flirting with temptation. Get out into the light and with bright and shining friends. Learn to say no to going to the places where temptation most often happens. You eliminate most of the need to say no. And that, too, is a positive witness to your friends.

"No" is something you have to say for yourself. You make your choices. Parents can't say it for you. God won't. You have to decide what kind of person you will be. It's your choice. As a matter of fact it's only your choice. Winners make it. They decided to do what's right.

Thoughts, dreams, and masturbation

Over the last few years I have received a lot of notes about involuntary sexual thoughts, sexual dreams, and masturbation. I know the concern about these issues is real. When I speak about them, no matter the group's age, the room gets very quiet. I'd like to share my best insight on all three. It must be *my* insight because in reading Scripture there is very little direct comment on those subjects. There are clear sexual principles offered but little comment—and no specific words—on that which troubles so many fine children of God. That's where we need to start: children of God. Be clear. These three things trouble a lot of children of God *and* even though they are troubled they are still children of God!

Dreams and thoughts are the more complicated of these three items. They are essentially involuntary. Every young adult moving toward sexual maturity, male or female, is daily surprised by all kinds of new and seemingly inexplicable sensations in their body. Certain areas of their body are very sensitive and seem to become increasingly so. Those areas produce sexual responses that are not only disturbing but often very pleasing! Sights, sounds, and even thoughts that pop up out of nowhere stimulate inner sexual sensations. When those things happen to you, it doesn't mean that you are impure or "dirty." It means you are human and developing. Recognize what stimulates you and focus on how to handle those moments.

One way to take control of the involuntary, inner, sexual churning is by consciously thinking about something else. If you are stimulated by a movie or a picture or a book, decide whether that's where you want to be or what you want in your mind. Busy yourself. These great teen years are God's gift to you for developing *all* that you are and have. When strange thoughts pop onto your conscious level, decide to act. They can often be shooed away. In their fully developed state they will encourage you to marry. That's the way things are supposed to be.

Dreams are another matter. I don't understand them. Even those who have much insight into dreams seem to know relatively little about them. I look at sexual dreaming the same way I look at my other involuntary appetites. They just are. I am caught up in the experience of them. I try to keep my life positive, but they happen.

Masturbation is not like an involuntary dream or thought. That makes it different. Years ago I was taught all kinds of evil things happen to people who masturbate. If the threat were true, most people would be doomed because at one time or another most people have masturbated. Start with that. It's a common part of life, but is it wrong?

I believe so. I believe it is wrong because it takes the sexual climax that was designed as a shared experience for two and makes it a "selfish" act by one. That doesn't seem right to me. All this happens in an intentional context of sexual fantasizing. The person on whom you sexually focus is "used" without their knowledge or will. That doesn't seem right to me. My final reason for thinking it is wrong is that people who talk about masturbation do so with a reserve and reluctance that seems to flow from an inner sense about the inappropriateness of it all. For some the very sexuality of it may be clearly opposed in Scripture. I'm not that sure. The God who is so explicit on homosexuality, lesbianism, rape, adultery, incest, fornication, and a multitude of other abuses is strangely silent on masturbation. Maybe God hopes we would be able to make an intelligent, spiritual, and proper decision in this matter. I believe I have. Each person will have to work out their best understanding of masturbation in the context of their own life.

I also know that prayer is of great benefit. Prayers that ask God to take away all sexuality are not going to be very successful. Why would the giver of our sexuality want to destroy it? But what about a prayer that asks God to give us a good and clean understanding of our maleness and femaleness. And ask him to help you focus your life on positive areas that so obviously bless and bring relief.

In an earlier age—with a life expectancy of 25 or 30—you might not have the masturbation problem. You would have been married at 14 or 15 and sexually active. But life preparations (and benefits—it evens out) are different now. Life expectancies are greater now; life possibilities are fuller now. We can't live in an age where we aren't. *This* is our day. We must strive to live in these days in the best way we know how: (1) to the glory of God, (2) for our neighbor's welfare, (3) in our own interest. Think and pray. And when you get done with that, pray and think.

Life-limiting decisions

Turn with me to the second big, "new" area of teenage notes and letters which surfaced since first we wrote in the early 1970s: life-limiting decisions. It's a fact. Today you are faced with a whole series of life-limiting decisions. Specifically you must decide about smoking, alcohol, and drugs. All are life limiting.

I'm not going to say much about drugs. Teens today have been clearly taught the facts about that subject. I doubt if I could add anything to what you already know. You know that drugs are another of life's clear-cut choices. Losers say yes to drugs. Winners say no.

Smoking and alcohol worry me, though. I'm not sure the choices are as clearly understood by teenagers. Don't concentrate exclusively on smoking and lung cancer. Instead read up on smoking and emphysema. Check out smoking and pneumonia, especially when someone has been in an accident and is forced to lie on their back in the hospital for lengths of time. The pressure that puts on nicotine-encrusted lungs! All the evidence ties smoking to so many problems. Weigh the decision. The consequences are substantial and immediate.

And drinking? There's plenty of information on that subject, too. One of the recurring letters I get from teens reads, "Why does my dad drink so much?" Alateens, Alanon, and a load of other organizations make the point: drinking is a complex and dangerous problem. It has an enormous antisocial spinoff. Drinking and driving remain a serious teenage problem. Would to God that one year's high school graduation season could pass without the sorry story of a carload of teenagers (driver drunk) slaughtered on the highway. Just as bad is when the carload of teens was not drinking but was victimized by the drunken driver of the car which plowed into them head-on. Drinking is a decision. Going where drinking takes place is a decision, too. Getting into the car of a drinking driver is a decision, too. Call home, first. Call somebody. Walk if you have to. All those are decisions, too. Decide what's life-expanding about drinking, and listen to yourself.

The ultimate limiter

But there is an ultimate life-limiter. It is called suicide. I can't think of anything more pointless than suicide. I just grieve. I'm sure there are many reasons a person takes their life. High on the list has to be low self-esteem—a loser mentality. But how could that be? God didn't enliven anyone to be a loser. That determination is self-inflicted. Low self-esteem is sometimes encouraged by society, or family, or friends. But in the final sense it's self-inflicted. Someone decides that their life is not worth living. Is there anything more tragic than that? But what can we do about it?

One recognition that has surfaced from study of teen suicides is that grieving survivors tend to romanticize the suicide's pointless death. We see it as a loving action that flowed from a broken heart. Were her parents so unreasonable that she had to make this statement? Did he die because he was unable to satisfy a demanding inner drive for excellence? In your private conversations with friends (or yourself) give that reasoning it's proper name: nonsense. If you don't, some unwary and weaker listener may think it all makes sense *and begin to plan their own death.*

Nothing is solved by suicide. Nothing. No one is "punished" by killing yourself. There's no revenge in it. As a matter of fact, most other people don't even remember it happened—except those who deserve the pain the least, and who really cared the most. Tell yourself and your friends, "If someone needs changing its better done by you live than you dead!" Take a stance on that issue.

Look out for depression and depressed friends. Both can be helped. The best help you can give is urge your depressed friends to get professional help. Take some initiative. Talk to the counselor, your pastor, a teacher. Share your provable concerns with their parents, their friends, the people they trust. Take an active position. Do it first of all with them. Do it secondly, if necessary, for them. Don't let their no-to-life decision happen without their hearing your yes-to-the-future response! Invite them to join you on a different path; a more exciting walk. Take them with you into the next chapter for a walk with God.

That's where we need to go in all this—back to the one who started it all. Let's go back to the Creator and hear of God's best intentions for us all.

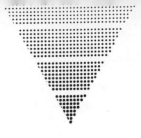

Nine

WALKING WITH GOD

I suspect that some who read this book will be looking for the map to achieving a successful life. Lots of cars. Lots of promotions. Lots of money. Lots of good times. We won't knock that agenda but our purpose in writing *Thank God I'm a Teenager* is larger and greater than that. Much larger. Much greater. We want to help you live the fullest Christian life possible.

The Christian motivation for wanting to get the most out of life comes from a belief that life doesn't belong to you. It is not yours or mine to manage as we choose. Life—all life— is God's possession. Paul the apostle saw it that way. He explains, "You are not your own; you were bought at a price. Therefore honor God with your body" (1 Cor. 6:19b, 20). In those two verses Paul points to three key understandings about life, including yours.

The first thing the apostle Paul claims is what we have already stated: God owns all life. The second is that your life is so valuable that God was willing to buy it. (We know the real truth is that he was willing to buy it *back* from the one who took it: Satan.) The third understanding is that we are to glorify God in the use of the body he has given us. In short: God claims you, all of you. God's claiming includes, but is not limited to, your talent, your physique, your home, your family, your money, your time, your faith, your fun, your friends, your hope, your peace. Everything.

How come?

What gives God the right to such a claim? I find that question best answered in Scripture. Start with that early recitation in Genesis 1 and 2. *God* created. It's his. It's all his.

Then soak yourself in the grand words of Psalm 139. Listen. Hear God say that he has willed from the day the foundation of the earth was laid (That long!) that you should be his. In that determination God made sure you were released from the kidnapping power of Satan through the forgiveness earned by Christ Jesus (Eph. 1:4). The Word tells us God has called us to faith by the Holy Spirit and given his redeemed ones the capacity to say, "Jesus is Lord" (1 Cor. 12:3). All that is in the past. Today God guides us by his presence and keeps us safe under the care of his angel messengers (Ps. 91:11). In God's tomorrow a place is reserved for each of us in heaven (John 14:2). That's not all. There's more.

God's Word tells us that before any of us have even discovered a problem and asked for help, God has already packaged the answer we need and sent it on its way (Isa. 65:24). Every day God gives us the power to resist the temptations of Satan and to stay on the safe way of life (James 4:7-8). God is so concerned about each one of us that, for reasons only he would understand but which we can all appreciate, the very hairs on our head are numbered (Matt. 10:30). The One who is that concerned with you isn't about to give you up—not even to yourself. You are God's: created, redeemed, sanctified. Just like the Apostles' Creed says.

Be aware of your contract

Some athletes complain that the professional contracts they sign are too restrictive. They claim they didn't want to give up as much control of their lives as their agreement specifies. Ha! They ought to check the "contract" all Christians have with God. Talk about tight! While God liberally gives us breath, forgiveness, and a new life in Christ, God also expects us to live up to the conditions of his contract. (Another Bible name for that contract is *covenant*.) But listen to this: even when we fail to live up to our promise God still keeps his part of the agreement. The contract/covenant which was prepared before your birth, and put in force at your Baptism, will never be changed by God. God keeps his word. He has agreed to be your God, help you toward freedom, broaden your horizons, give you cause for joy, fill your life with wonder, and assure you of every good gift *as long as you will let him*. The only thing that terminates God's contract is your decision (remember what that means—"to cut") to reject it. How do we know that? God said so—in creation, in his handling of history, in the gift of Christ. And God says so in his written revelation, the Scripture.

A lot of what you decide about the words in this book will depend on whether you believe the Scripture of God—its commands and its promises; its direction and its instructions; its correctives and its assurances; its central story of redemption—is true. You must decide. You must. And you will, even if you decide to not decide. That, too, is a decision. It carries with it the fullest consequences any decision has. Proper choices based on a solid belief that God speaks to us in his Word will make all the difference in the world for you—this world and the next.

You certainly realize that when I bring up decisions I'm not just referring to the decisions about personal conduct we developed in the last chapter. I have more in mind than that. I'm deeply concerned whether you believe that "God was reconciling the world to himself in Christ, not counting man's sins against them" (2 Cor. 5:19). It is incredibly important that you make up your mind whether God's Word is true not only in matters of conduct but also in its teaching that Jesus earned forgiveness for you *and makes it available to you at the very moment you sin—even if you are committing the same sin for the 197th time.* Sunday school students know that is true. At least they know it in their heads. But do you accept it in your heart as God's Spirit-given truth through his Word? I hope so. Good decisions, whether in matters of conduct or commitments of faith, demand that inner conviction.

Christ's body, the church

As the truths of the Christian faith move from "head truth" to "heart beliefs" you develop both in your faith and your life. Your world changes. It really changes. You treat people differently. You see your responsibilities differently. You judge daily occurrences differently. Right? It's something like that in your world of church membership, too.

Are you a church member right now? A Lutheran? Methodist? Presbyterian? Roman Catholic? Some other? Are you active? Maybe you attend if, when, and where your family attends. Or do you answer the question about church membership by claiming the nearest church to your home. Most teens pick and choose through the alternatives I have suggested. Their commitment to church and their level of denominational loyalty is quite low. Will it change? Possibly. It will depend on a choice. For many teens one day there comes the decision to really join a church. Really. If that is an inner determination to become a functioning part of the church you attend, great things will happen. One of the first, and the nicest, things that happen is that not only will you belong to a church but it will also belong to you. You become a part of it. It becomes a part of you. Your choice expresses your deepest convictions. It's a family decision.

I have watched many teenagers go through that experience. In a very real sense that decision to become active and involved is the moment they first "joined" a church. While many had technically become members of a congregation years before, it was only when they realized what membership meant, and chose to really join, that they became vital parts of a congregational family of faith. What a wonderful thing! I hope it happens to you. When it does be careful. I need to caution you about something that could happen next *through* you.

Don't be a church pusher

Some who took years to develop a personal understanding of their salvation, their faith, their relationship to Christ, and their membership in a congregation become "church pushers." They turn right around and want to force others to believe as they believe. But instantly. They become pushy—shoving religion down the throats of their friends. They even get upset at any apparent lack of response. That's so odd. They know force didn't work on them. Why do they try to force others?

There is a better way. Let the Spirit do God's saving work—like he planned. We then can do what we are called to do: witness to our faith, but patiently. Hasn't God been patient with us? Your journey to faith did not take place overnight. It didn't happen because someone forced their belief on you. If anyone believes it's because God gives faith. He does the working in you. People like you and me are the bearers of the Word, but it is always God working through the Word who brings about conversion and faith. Let God do the pushing— when he wants. In the meanwhile focus on yourself and your journey of faith. Notice any differences? Look closely.

Just as your body changes as you grow up, so your faith changes as it matures. Both happen gradually, one step at a time. From one week to another you may not see a significant difference in your physical development, or in your faith. Yet there is growth. Everyone goes through the "growing" described in Chapter 1. They grow constantly, at a slow but steady rate.

How does growth happen? Spiritual growth happens as you "eat" the spiritual food God has prepared and offers to you. That spiritual food includes Christ's body and blood in Communion, God's Word and the spiritual experiences he brings to you. God intends that you grow and keep on growing. God intends that with each passing period of life you achieve new levels of Christian perception. The Bible speaks of "reaching out," "growing up," and "maturing in your faith." It will happen to you if you let it.

Worship

Worship is one way God helps you grow. If you commit yourself to worship at least once a week you will grow. But first you have to get over the "I-hate-church" attitude that some people carry from their childhood. I got over it the day I understood what I meant when I was saying, "I don't get anything out of church." I didn't mean that there was nothing in church to be received. I meant I didn't understand that giving, not getting, is the key. My complaint really meant I wasn't giving. I had to learn that the way to get things is by giving. Give nothing—get nothing. Give something—get much.

Worship, the word we use for Sunday morning activity, means "to serve." If I'm going to worship, I'm going to serve. Serving, in turn, means I'll have to work. I'm not working when I'm lying on my back in bed, gabbing in the back row of the sanctuary, or goofing off in the basement. Work is a very active thing. So is worship. You can't stare at the cover of the hymnal and learn a song. You can't get insights about God from an unopened and unused Bible. You must put yourself into the worshiping experience. Sit up. Pay attention. Work at understanding. Give of yourself.

The many faces of serving

Serving also means doing things in the worship service. Have you thought about singing in the choir? Ushering? Planning a worship experience? Playing a musical instrument?

Folding the bulletins? Reading the lessons? Composing a prayer? Think about those things. Act on your thoughts! There's more.

Make a prayer list and take it to church with you. Include on your prayer list friends who have needs, problems that need solving in our world, personal hopes and dreams. In church, in the company of other Christians, do private praying—but include your concerns in your public prayers as well. Pray for people by name. Take them from your heart and lay them on the heart of the Lord. When you start praying with power and a purpose you realize why Jesus broke out in sweat that night in the garden when he brought his yearnings to the Father. Prayer requires intensity plus concentration. It calls for involvement and effort.

It's also important that you bring your Christian life under intentional control. Decide to read a portion of Scripture every day. You can do that. Commit yourself to prayer before and after meals. Set aside a specific portion of your income as a weekly offering. Decisions like those make what used to be dull very exciting.

My pastor

Not many pastors think they are serving teenagers very well. They aren't sure what they can and ought to do. I think many are even afraid of their younger sisters and brothers. Pastors tell me that teenagers don't say much to them. They say that's why they don't know how teenagers feel about things. Pastors are not sure they communicate with teenagers—or whether they know how to. But when I talk with teenagers I discover that pastors actually communicate very well. Teenagers hear what their pastor has to say and treasure pastoral insight and advice. I do have to say that not many teenagers express their feelings to their pastor very clearly! They seem as reluctant to comment, commend, or compliment as their pastor is to reach and share. So why not do something about it?

Why don't you decide to have a talk with your pastor? Do it right. Make an appointment. Organize our thoughts. Tell your pastor how you feel about things and what makes you happy. Share your pains, your hopes, and your desires. If you don't understand some things in church, use that triple-E method I described in a previous chapter. Speak up. If the prayers in church make little sense to you, say, "Pastor, the prayers in church sound funny. They don't make much sense to me. Because I don't understand them my mind drifts and I feel like I'm a hypocrite." Your pastor may change the prayers, or maybe help you change your level of understanding. Best of all he might ask your help. It could happen! Go a step further: volunteer to help around the church. Try to catch the pastor's vision of things. When you understand that, you may have a clearer picture of what you could be doing at church to help him, help others, and help yourself.

Your pastor has a significant office. Called to preach the Word, administer Baptism and the Lord's Supper, and lead to the forgiveness of sins those who repent, your pastor has help to offer at many levels of life. Your pastor wants to hear from you. Speak up. Give your pastor a chance to help you, especially with three great decisions of life.

Three great decisions

The three most important decisions anyone makes in life first pop up during the teenage years. As the years pass the decisions, and their implications, mount higher and higher until they dominate your horizon. The decisions? (1) What kind of person will I be; (2) What kind of vocation will I seek; (3) What kind of person will I choose to marry. You won't finalize those decisions in your teenage years, but you will inevitably take important first steps toward facing those questions well before your 20th birthday. The questions often come to you in the sequence I listed.

In the first phase of your journey through life the number

one question is experimenting with and then deciding what kind of person you will be. Positive? Social? Concerned? Selfish? Cooperative? Sensitive? Aggressive? And other characteristics. In the earliest stages of maturing you are working with those possibilities for yourself. You may change later, but the pattern you first select will be with you a long time. That's something to pray about. Let God help you decide what kind of individual you want to be.

In the second period, based somewhat on the kind of person you decide you want to become, you will move toward a decision about what kind of vocation you will follow through life. Service? Sales? Teaching? Business? And lots more. Just as important as the "what" of your primary vocational decision is the "why." Check out your "why." It may be a worthy "why," but it may also be a selfish one. And, as you will discover, your vocational decision is closely related to the kind of person you decided you want to be.

Third, during the teen years you are going to develop a sense about whom you may want to marry. You may not discover a specific person, but you will determine a type. At the same time you will begin to think about what you expect to bring to marriage, and what you expect to find in a marriage. These expectations shape your thinking as you decide when you want to get married, who your specific marriage partner will be, and how you then want to live with one another. And, of course, there is another real possibility. You may intentionally determine that marriage is not desirable to you. That's an OK choice, too. Like all other decisions the final determination of how good your decision is depends on how you made it.

At the heart of each of your key early decisions is the question of how you feel about yourself, about others, and about God. That means those decisions are religious decisions. If God is alive in your life, he will be with you as you make those decisions and you will see them through the eyes of God. Those eyes will help you see yourself, your strengths, your weaknesses, and God's power to do in you what needs doing. God helps his children grasp the things that have lasting value and that really count.

Hans Lilje, imprisoned by Hitler in World War II, once said that a primary task of the church to its members is to help them realize that at the heart of every decision in life is a religious question. Then he added, "Once that is recognized the church must help her members think." I agree with that. Based on thousands of notes and letters we have already received we know that the ideas and Christian ideals in this book will make the concerned teenager feel God's questions—and think. No serious book about growing will teach absolute responses to cover every situation. We haven't tried. How could that be possible? Every one of us is different.

But we have tried to give you useful tools for facing life's choices. It is our prayer that you use them in the spirit they were offered: to the glory of God and for the good of others. Believe us, it's exciting and wonderful being a teenager and having the opportunity to struggle through your questions looking for God's best answers. It's almost as exciting and wonderful being the teenager's friend during this growing time.

Thanks

Neither of us wants to be a teenager, again. It was fun once. Now we're busy with the later adult years. From our perspective we can tell you that great and exciting things are coming your way. Ours, too. None of us needs to worry—or hurry. Every age has its blessings. Work at and enjoy the unique experiences God has reserved for the seven years between 12 and 20. One day at a time—God's way—they will get you ready for what's coming to you.

In the meanwhile think of us. We're on the same road with you, just a few days ahead. Our feet are planted in God's today. Our eyes, with yours, are on God's tomorrow. We both can have confidence about the distant future because of God's yesterday. As we offer you this book of help our prayer is: "Heavenly Father, give every young person who moves through their glorious early years eyes of understanding, a heart full of your love, a life filled with satisfaction, and the grace to say, 'Thank God I'm a teenager.' Lead them to praise your name for the handful of years you have already given them and hope for more of the same. Move them to honor you for their faith in Christ. Empower them to live in his love and lead others to your promise of life both now and eternally. Amen."

P.S. Much of what we added came as a result of your written suggestions, questions and comments. We always try to answer our mail. That's not always possible. But we do read and treasure everything you send. We look forward to hearing more from you.